SKIRTS AT WAR

BEYOND DIVORCED MOM/STEPMOM CONFLICT

by
Jennifer Newcomb Marine and Jenna Korf
(with Mario Korf)

Published by Nest Press.

ISBN-10: 1491268964
ISBN-13: 978-1491268964

Edited by Jeanne Goshe and Amy Eye

Designed by damonza.com
Cover Design by damonza.com

Printed in the United States of America.

For information about special sales and corporate purchases, please contact Jennifer Newcomb Marine or Jenna Korf at JenandJenna@noonesthebitch.com.

For more hands-on support, please join us online at SkirtsAtWar.com and NoOnesTheBitch.com. We'd love to have you join our Facebook pages, workshops and private forum. Jenna Korf is available for private coaching at StepmomHelp.com or JennaKorf.com. You can keep up with Jennifer Newcomb Marine's latest projects at JenniferNewcombMarine.com.

CONTENTS

Join Our Community!. v
Introduction. vi

SECTION ONE: PROBLEMS

Chapter 1
Instincts: Why Is This Stuff So Hard? 3

Chapter 2
Support: Are You and Your Friends Actually Making It Worse? 25

Chapter 3
Men: What Does the Man in the Middle Think? 41

Chapter 4
Expectations: What Were You Assuming?. 51

Chapter 5
Self-Worth: Why Does This Make Me Feel So Lousy About Myself? . . . 67

Chapter 6
Boundaries: How Do I Keep Her Out of My Business? 81

SECTION TWO: POWER TOOLS

Chapter 7
Power Tools: How Can I Feel Better Right Now? 97

SECTION THREE: MAKING PROGRESS

Chapter 8
Instincts: Making Progress 125

Chapter 9
Support: Making Progress. 139

Chapter 10
Men: Making Progress 151

Chapter 11
Expectations: Making Progress 171

Chapter 12
Self-Worth: Making Progress 185

Chapter 13
Boundaries: Making Progress 197

Chapter 14
Conclusion & Other Resources 215

Thank You 219
Acknowledgements. 221
About the Authors. 223

JOIN OUR COMMUNITY!

If you'd like new friends by your side as you read this book and work through the material, consider becoming a part of our safe and secure online community at SkirtsAtWar.com

You'll find:
- encouragement
- answers to any questions you might have
- a private space to complete the quizzes and journal questions
- free PDFs
- ongoing new material

We hope to meet you at SkirtsAtWar.com!

INTRODUCTION

HOW DID THIS BOOK COME TO BE?

*S*kirts at War probably should have come before *No One's the Bitch: A Ten-Step Plan for Mothers and Stepmothers* (GPP Life, 2009), which was co-written by Jennifer Newcomb Marine and Carol Marine, the stepmom to her kids. While both books focus on humanizing the ex-wife or stepmom in your life and minimizing conflict, *Skirts at War* addresses the situation many of our readers *actually find themselves in*. It is almost impossible to consider making peace with "the enemy" when she's still pitching Molotov cocktails into your window at night, trying to burn your house down. (At least, that's how it feels.)

JENNIFER:

In many ways, this book is a response to the comments I received after co-writing No One's the Bitch *with Carol. "But you don't understand!" many women said, "Carol actually sounds normal, but the woman in my situation is batshit crazy!" I heard lengthy descriptions of harrowing problems with the other household that were completely over my head. I'd never dealt with such intense conflict in my own situation before. How could I possibly give advice to women who were drowning in conflict?*

Turns out, I could relate to their problems, but from a different vantage point. In overcoming some of the biggest challenges I've ever faced in the past several years, I've developed a new repertoire of skills for restoring equanimity to my life. I'll be drawing from those resources to help you regain your own inner stillness.

JENNA:

The most difficult aspect of my stepmom journey has been the dynamic between me and my stepchildren's mom. I never could have imagined that "dealing" with another person could be so challenging, but I'm living proof that you can find happiness while being bombarded with stress. In fact, my marriage is stronger than ever, in spite of the conflict that we continue to experience. I've found a way to make my life work, while coping with difficulties that I wouldn't wish on anyone. In this book I'll be sharing just how I did that.

Most step-parenting books barely mention the fraught dynamics between stepmom and ex-wife, and if they do, only dedicate a page or two to it. For a relationship that's causing thousands of women a life of misery and heartache, a full-length book is most definitely needed! When step-parenting books give stepmoms advice on the ex-wife, they usually don't describe how that advice might create a backlash. It's crucial for both stepmoms and moms to be aware of the dynamics between the two sides and how to calm the waters of conflict.

HOW IS IT DIFFERENT FROM THE FIRST ONE?

This book is about what *you* can do to help yourself if the mom or stepmom doesn't meet you halfway, as opposed to actively attempting to create a partnership, as encouraged in *No One's the Bitch*. We'll talk about how to identify and isolate the elements that are worsening the conflict (both inner and outer) and how to focus on the means *that are within your control* for creating peace.

This book is also different in that we are not "related" to each other, as Carol and Jennifer are by the marriage of Jennifer's ex-husband to Carol. We came together as business partners with complementary skills and perspectives in real life and online. Jenna helps Jennifer remember what it's like to have a divorced mom/stepmom relationship that's not necessarily harmonious, whereas Jennifer reminds Jenna that there's always hope for huge and surprising turnarounds.

WHAT'S IN IT FOR ME?

We're hoping this book will help you feel empowered again, but also better able to withstand ongoing discord between you and the other woman. You may not have chosen to share your life with her, but with your newfound tools and mindset, you'll be able to dodge the slings and arrows coming your way and avoid the wasted time and energy it takes to send them back to her.

Rather than triumphing *over* the divorced mom or stepmom, our goal is to get you to the point where you see her doing something irrational and hurtful and think, "Enh, there she goes again," as you shrug your shoulders and move on. Victory is not even *necessary as you learn to walk parallel to each other, grounded and unfazed.*

HOW SHOULD I USE IT?

The book has three main sections:

1. **Problem Areas** – an in-depth analysis of the most common trouble spots
2. **Power Tools** – strategies to help you cope in the moment and long-term
3. **Making Progress** – a positive vision of applying tools to the problems

JUMPING AROUND

Feel free to jump around in the book as needed, depending on which challenges are most urgent for you right now. Some sections may make more sense if you read them from beginning to end because we are building upon cumulative concepts.

If you need immediate, hands-on help, you are welcome to skip ahead to the corresponding chapter in *Making Progress* to imagine what it looks like to *get* somewhere. Hopefully, you will eventually be intrigued by the *Power Tools* to go back and read those too.

Do whatever works for you!

BECOMING AWARE OF YOUR THOUGHT PATTERNS

In each chapter of *Making Progress,* we've provided a resource called "Check Your Thinking." You'll find a list of possible negative, subconscious beliefs you may be carrying around and healthier, positive beliefs that can replace them, followed by meditation mantras to create deep, lasting change. In *Power Tools,* we explain why becoming aware of your subconscious thoughts is so important.

DO THE EXERCISES!

We've tried to make the book as interactive as possible because we know from experience that half of what you will learn comes from the material itself, half will come from considering how it applies to your own life, and half of its value will come from experimenting and putting your insights into practice.

Wait! *Three* halves? Yep. Welcome to the nutty world of divorce-connected families, where there are always too many sides to every story.

Let's jump into the cold water together!

SECTION ONE
PROBLEMS

CHAPTER 1

INSTINCTS: WHY IS THIS STUFF SO HARD?
(a messy reality vs. managing our natural reactions)

THE NEW NORMAL

It is six in the evening on a typical street in your neighborhood. Most adults are home from work, sitting down to dinner with their families. If you were to scan these families by the ages of their children, the preschoolers and elementary school-aged kids might live with both of their parents. The middle schoolers would most likely live with a single parent in one family and a stepparent in another. The high schoolers would almost certainly be living with a stepparent (perhaps unmarried) in each household.

While it's true divorce rates have dropped over the last decade (by one percentage point), most statistics don't take into account the age of the marriage itself. The longer a marriage exists, the more likely it is to dissolve. Unnerving, isn't it?

1,300 new stepfamilies form every day. There are now more stepfamilies in the United States than nuclear families, *though experts can't prove it*. How can that be? Amazingly, the U.S. Census Bureau does not count a stepfamily as such if it is not the child's primary residence, and the latest Census survey in 2010 didn't even *include* remarriage data. This is mind-boggling, given the 73 percent rate of divorce for stepfamilies. Apparently, it's just too hard to quantify stepfamilies these days, with co-habitating couples and so many families in flux.

A divorce rate of almost three out of every four stepfamilies is cause enough for alarm, but we should be concerned about the risks to stepfamilies for another reason. Whether the other household is headed by a single parent or is also a stepfamily, both families now form a connected "nest" for their children. We must ask ourselves, *Given this nest, are we parenting our children and stepchildren up to our own standards?* Is the conflict and tension between the two households interfering with our ability to love, guide and successfully launch our children into the world? Are we helping our kids become adults who are capable of doing the same with their own children later in life?

If you eavesdrop on stepmoms, ex-wives and single parents online, it's clear there is an enormous amount of trouble between the households. These are some of the most challenging familial configurations possible, but divorced moms and stepmoms are often oblivious to the biggest causes of their problems with each other:

- dual-household relationships trigger our deepest fears
- clashing instincts are confusing and wreak havoc upon our psyches
- our "emotional authority" prevents us from recognizing any interpretation of reality that differs from our own

In this chapter, we'll talk about why this is so. We will also show you a bird's-eye view of your situation and identify some hidden factors that may be adding to your stress.

Power Tools (Section Two) provides you with an overview of techniques designed to help you create change. In *Instincts: Making Progress* (Section Three), we'll walk you through tools you can apply to this particular issue to create lasting change for the better.

FEAR VS. LOVE: THE IMPACT ON YOUR FAMILY

One reason divorce-connected family relationships are so vitally important is because *we are either setting the stage for love in our families—or fear.* We are modeling how to resolve conflict with maturity and grace for our children—or how to negatively react to someone we do not understand. As authority figures, we are looking for opportunities throughout the day to increase feelings of closeness in our family through play, compassion and forgiveness—or we are keeping score and adding to our pile of resentments in the corner.

Our children's futures will closely resemble the way we live now. Are the current interactions between households what you would like for your children to replicate in their own lives, as married grown-ups?

Although it may seem counterintuitive, *Skirts at War* is about increasing love and connection in your own family, not necessarily *between* the two families. When you are less stressed, more relaxed, and not taking bad behavior so personally, the kids and your partner will likely follow suit. As you recognize how you have contributed to misunderstandings and drama between the two households and take responsibility for your own happiness, *your family* will also become happier, kinder and more open.

The fear goes down.

The love goes up.

Now, isn't *that* worth passing on as an inheritance? We think so.

IN THE WORDS OF OUR READERS

> **Zen (divorced mom, former stepmom):** "*I have to say that for me the most unnatural thing by far is being separated from your child for extended periods of time, and them having a life totally separate from you. I hated missing milestones with my children because they were with the other parent. I also find it incredibly difficult at times to have another person's values and parenting culture and the judgment of my values/parenting culture as a constant presence in my and my kids' lives.*"

> **Leila (stepmom):** "*In the beginning, my stepkids and I had about three years of "the honeymoon phase" where we just showered them with love in our home and they reciprocated. Then we went through two years of venomous hatred from my stepson that nearly tore us apart. We got good coaching and have recovered and my stepson has come out of his dark phase, but I will never be the same. My heart has been so wounded.*"

> **Kelli N. (divorced mom):** "*I'm surprised at all the emotions still attached to certain situations. You'd think after the dissolving of*

a relationship with the dad, mean words wouldn't affect you. But somehow, even after all these years, they can bring you just as down as they did when you were still together."

A.M. (stepmom): "Hardest thing I've ever done. *False accusations, stepdaughter lies to the mom about so many things because that's what the mom wants to hear. I feel like everyone's negative emotions are blamed on me. I'm the only one that has to 'do better' when the ones that are failing the stepkids are Mom and Dad (they are really high conflict). Yet I'm the only one that gets thrown under the bus. It's such a heavy burden to bear. I can honestly say I had no idea what I was getting into."*

Let's take an inventory. Which of the categories below are you in? What about your ex-husband and his partner? His ex-wife and her partner? Friends and family?

Our Dual-Family Categories	Divorced (or never married) mom	Stepmom
You have kids of your own from your divorce or partnership, your partner has none	hers	–
Your male partner has kids from previous marriage and you have kids together	–	his and ours
Your male partner has children from a previous marriage	hers and his	his
You and your childless, divorced partner in your stepfamily have also had children	hers and ours	–
You and your partner have had children, in addition to the kids you both have from your divorces	his, hers and ours	–

JENNIFER NEWCOMB MARINE AND JENNA KORF

Imagine all the overlapping lines between family members in our dual-family (or tri-family) situations, like a map in an airline magazine showing all the places they fly to. Don't forget about extended family, step in-laws—and because of the high rate of divorce for stepfamilies—*former* stepmoms, stepdads and stepchildren. If we are, in actuality, *surrounded* by complex family groupings, then why are we still regarding our reconstituted families as an aberration, a surprise? Why are we taking each dual-family problem one maddening drip at a time, without an informed overview of the most common challenges that we all face—and more importantly, their solutions?

This is life now, *for most of us!* That's the first wake-up call.

Our family situations aren't just some temporary pit stop on our way back to normality. This *is* the New Normal. This matters because way too many of us are absolutely miserable, doing the dog paddle out in the middle of the ocean, desperately wishing for a tanker churning through the water to scoop us up, bearing warm, dry towels and hot coffee.

We cannot guarantee a cruise ship rescue for each and every reader, but we are hoping this book will help you to reach land. Preferably Fiji or Bali. With lots of great food, a hut in the shade, Mai Tais and plenty of good friends who *get it*.

They are out there. Potentially millions of them.

GOING AGAINST OUR INSTINCTS

The second wake-up call is this: these relationships are so damned difficult because *nature didn't intend them to be this way.*

The last thing a mother imagines when she's pregnant (such excitement and anticipation!) is that she may someday have to share her babies (or their father) with another woman—even if she and her husband can't stand each other by the time they divorce.

And when a woman falls in love with a man and gets married, the last thing she's thinking is that she'll be okay having her partner remain inextricably connected to another woman he's no longer committed to, especially since he's now married to *her*.

Children are expecting to take their cues from the same, lifelong, primary caregivers. Fathers and mothers are *supposed* to stay together to raise their dependent young until they're ready to leave the nest, eighteen years later.

For both women, the presence of the other just feels *wrong*. Yet we're forced to accept a situation that goes against the very fiber of our being, and do it with good manners, flexibility and smiles on our faces. Fat chance.

IN THE WORDS OF OUR READERS

> **Christine O. (stepmom):** *"I have my stepson in my house full time and I have to remember to step back, which goes against my maternal side. I want to jump in and help where I would want my own child to have help, but then I have to remember for the greater good and peace that he's not mine. It isn't my place to jump in—or I need to give his parents the chance, but then it drives me insane when they don't. And it isn't that I necessarily think they're doing it wrong, but it just isn't how I might do it. I care very deeply for my stepson and want what's best for him, but it can be hard to face that I don't get to decide what that may be."*

> **Kelli N. (divorced mom):** *"For me, it's unnatural to hand my daughter to another women to help raise her. When you are pregnant, you read all these stories and tips on how to raise a child. You try and do everything right— feed her healthy foods, shower her with love. Nowhere in those books does it tell you how to 'share' your child with another 'bonus Mom.' You are thrown into a situation when the dad meets another woman that you do not know. You did not invite her into your life, or trust her to do what's best for your child. I don't think anything in this world is more unnatural than that!"*

> **Meg (stepmom):** *"It's unnatural to have a woman who openly hates me be so involved in every aspect of my life. It's unnatural to not be able to be myself, open, loving, goofy, etc., out of fear of stealing the mom's thunder. It's unnatural that I don't get to make decisions with my husband. I have to include his ex in a lot of daily decisions."*

Shannan W. (divorced mom): *"I think it feels so unnatural to have my parenting questioned in a way it never was before. Until Stepmom came into the picture, Dad thought I was a good mother. Over the years, everything I did from how I dressed my stepdaughter, what I fed her, what she watched on television, even whether she walked home from school or not was measured, quantified, and then judged as moral character flaws. I just felt like nothing I ever did as a parent was going to be good enough, even though it was good enough before. I had to justify and explain every action, not necessarily to them, but to myself, because I knew someone was 'watching.' I didn't feel like I could parent naturally, at least for many years."*

Renee S. (stepmom): *"The hardest part is balancing the interests of all the kids. The mom only has to worry about her kids. She has to make sure they are fed, clothed, and that their financial future is secure. While I am as deeply invested in their future as my husband is, I also have to look out for my biological children who have half as many resources as their sisters."*

Jean L. (divorced mom, stepmom): *"I am currently visiting my father-in-law and his companion of 20 years, so I am seeing things perhaps the way my stepkids view me. When there is someone who has been added to the family later and the stepkids are older, it has become quite clear to me how little that step's presence matters. Not that there isn't caring, but just that many things about the step are 'irrelevant' because there is no common ground: history, relationship, etc. That is why my stepkids don't engage when I bring up something from my past or my family, and why they don't engage with me about my day, why they feel so strongly about me 'just not being there' some of the times, and why they look at me strange when I mention something about my son (who does not live with us). I just don't matter a good part of the time. As my husband, his sister and aunt struggle also in managing dynamics regarding*

*my father-in-law's companion, I see how similar my feelings are
with my stepchildren toward me."*

SET UP TO FAIL

As our reader's comments illustrate, the two households can become one of the
biggest challenges *for each other*. Would it make you feel any better to know
these situations are fundamentally flawed? It's true.

Our divorce-connected families can bring out the worst in us. They stir up
our most primitive fears about not belonging and losing our power. They activate
our secret terrors of feeling abandoned and unlovable, of being treated unfairly,
of having our insecurities laid bare for all the world to see. It's as if control
that rightfully belongs in *our* hands has been wrenched away. The other person
who is upsetting us is not only overreaching, they're doing it all wrong! Now,
a total *stranger* can trump the choices we make and the influence we have with
those we love the most. If you understand *how*, then you'll understand *why* you
sometimes find yourself behaving like someone you don't even recognize, despite
your best efforts to rise above it all. You'll start to understand why things that
seem so *normal* to you automatically offend the other woman or household.

There is the widespread sense of something going very wrong today in family
life on the whole. Home is supposed to be our place of refuge; a place where
you are unconditionally loved and accepted. Where you can let down your guard
and recharge from the stresses of the world.

There are consequences to going against the grain of *biologically* motivated
expectations, but they can be tempered. The good news is that it *is* possible to
reduce the impact of unpleasant situations beyond your control through foresight
and advanced preparation.

But we're getting ahead of ourselves... First, a little bit more about us and
why we understand where you are right now.

IN JENNA'S WORDS

When I met my husband, I was thirty-five and divorced (with no kids). I had
done the whole "self-discovery" thing, spent time with a great therapist, read

a ton of self-improvement books, and in my opinion, accomplished some real emotional growth. I wasn't looking for my "other half." *I* was my other half. I didn't have a void that needed filling. I finally felt whole. And I was looking for a partner to forge a healthy relationship with. I had faced my demons and was flourishing. I thought I was set.

My parents divorced when I was seven and they couldn't have handled it better. They never fought in front of me and my brother or spoke negatively about each other. On top of that awesomeness, my mom and stepmom had always been friendly and got along well. That's what was modeled for me. That was the norm. Wasn't it?

So when I met my husband, I assumed his ex-wife would like me, appreciate me and be thankful he had met someone with a good head on her shoulders. I mean, really, what's not to like! Turns out I was a little off in my assumption.

Fast-forward three years. My relationship with my husband was wonderful. Being with him was the easiest thing I'd ever done. But dealing with his ex was the *hardest*. I'd never been in such a contentious relationship. In the past, whenever I was confronted with someone with whom I just could not regularly agree, I cut them out of my life. But you can't very well do that in these situations. I was stuck.

I kept thinking if I was just nicer or more open, it would get better, but it didn't. It felt like everything I did was scrutinized under a microscope. It got to the point where I dreaded the sound of a text message and got queasy at the thought of checking my email. It's easy to focus on the one negative thing in your life and this was mine. I just wanted peace and quiet, but it was nowhere to be found. By the way, don't let anyone tell you these situations aren't physically traumatic. I'm pretty sure I still experience a degree of Post-Traumatic Stress Disorder every time I hear the sound of an incoming text message on my husband's phone!

Finding peace in this situation was about a couple of different things. One, my husband. He protected me by setting boundaries whenever possible. Our marriage became stronger and I focused on that. And two, I'm a big fan of the belief that we're only responsible for our own actions and emotions. I finally looked at the situation and said, "I'm not responsible for her. I can't control the assumptions she makes about me or how she interprets my words, intentions or actions. I can't even control how she interprets the *facts* of a situation." We all see life through the filter of our own experiences, and hers were very different than mine.

We each have our own path. I had to do my own healing and not wait for her to change. I do my best to protect myself from what I perceive as attacks, but I also remain open to things one day improving with her.

IN JENNIFER'S WORDS

Now that my relationship with Carol and David (my kids' stepmom and my ex) is mostly good, I'll bet most people think I can't relate to the issues that divorced moms and stepmoms face anymore. Not so.

Starting in 2008, I had three successive years that were worse than anything I'd ever experienced, even harder than adapting to a divorce. While I knew in my *bones* I had a contribution to make to divorced families and stepfamilies with my first book, I made one mistake after another based on a heartfelt gamble. My leap of faith didn't pay off, at least not in the way I was hoping.

I was humbled and amazed that the book had changed lives (based on the feedback we got), but I was still going financially backwards. I desperately wanted to be of service, based on life lessons I'd learned the hard way. I also wanted to please others, to be liked and respected. I felt obligated to help readers of the book and blog; to spend hours on email and Facebook, brainstorming solutions to women's urgent, complicated problems and to write comprehensive blog posts in response. I took it personally when people publicly complained about wanting more free support online. When I tried to go back to getting a regular job, the economy had dramatically changed. Despite my best efforts, I couldn't get one.

Overwhelmed by external pressures that I couldn't control, I reverted to old, automatic patterns and became locked in a downward spiral of shame and fear. Stressed beyond belief and unable to sleep, I had heart palpitations from anxiety and more migraines than ever. I couldn't enjoy hanging out with family and friends (nor could I afford to do anything fun with them). I forgot what my own laugh sounded like. Rather than holding my head high after writing a book that had truly helped some families, I felt like a total failure, a feeling so at odds with what I was trying to put out there into the world

When I finally reached my breaking point, I surprised myself by selling my house, leaving a city and friends I loved and moving across the country to reinvent myself. After some intense inner work, I can honestly say I'm happier now than I've ever been. In this book, I'll use some of the same tricks and tools I learned to help you create your own peace. I hope you find healing here, just as I have in the last two years of my life.

Alright, enough about us. Onward!

WHO GETS MORE "EMOTIONAL AUTHORITY?"

One day while we were talking on the phone, we realized that one reason dual-household families can seem so *impossible* is because we have the two most important relationships of our lives competing against each other: parent and child versus husband and wife. This creates a dynamic in relationships that we like to call "emotional authority."

Family members often feel like the *strength* of their bonds to other family members automatically confers upon them certain rights, certain "givens." The intensity and purity of your love for another seems to equal more power, more say in what happens to them. It's as if that person is "yours," even though on the surface that sounds ridiculous. We're already familiar with how this works in "traditional" relationships, especially in nuclear families.

Think about it. When you were growing up, your mother (or primary care-taker) was typically the one directing your life: making decisions about what you would do, eat, when you would sleep, play with friends, health-related issues, schooling, etc.

Just as in nature, we accept as an instinctual "given" that your mother or caretaker would protect you against any perceived threats, such as bullies in school, grumpy neighbors or extended family members who might not have your best interests at heart—all in an effort to nurture and love you, without giving her actions a second thought. Granted, some of us didn't grow up in nurturing households and suffered at the hands of neglectful or abusive parents, but nevertheless, we know the archetype well.

As a society, we also have certain *givens* for a husband-and-wife relationship. Spouses and cohabiting romantic partners confide in each other about the most intimate matters. Traditionally, they make financial decisions together, divvy up household chores, and do their best to form a consensus on parenting values. They are loyal to each other and sexually monogamous. They protect their right to dictate what happens in their household. They relax together, pick up the slack for each other, and rest in the safety of knowing their partner has their back as they weather the stresses of life.

But let's cross the loyalty lines a bit and see what happens.

Let's say the stepmom is largely responsible for overseeing her stepchild's homework in her home as dad works full-time and is less available. She knows her stepson has been struggling in school after witnessing many nights of home-work that ended in tears. For the past two years, mom, dad and stepmom have all had access to the child's teachers and school records. But suddenly, seemingly out of nowhere, mom revokes stepmom's privileges and lets the school know that she no longer wants the stepmom involved. The stepmom is thinking, "What the hell? I've already been at this for two years now. Furthermore, my husband wants me to help, so that's reason enough to be involved." Meanwhile, the mom is thinking "It's the *father's* job to stay on top this, not the stepmom's. Who does she think she is? Why do we need one more person complicating everything? She needs to just let the parents handle this and step out of it!"

Believe it or not, the stepmom feels all the mother tiger instincts that a *mother* would normally feel. What happens when the mom tries to pull rank with a stepmom who feels just as connected and concerned about her stepson as she would her own son? Fireworks!

As for the mom, she remembers when it was just herself and her ex handling school matters. They had separate parent-teacher conferences so they wouldn't have to be in the same room. Now there's another woman who feels like she "has the right" to be included in communications with her child's teacher. Mom tried to go with the flow and be respectful, but she's had enough. She's supposed to be endlessly flexible? Says who?

It certainly seems as if one side is always the winner or the loser in our divorce-connected families. A huge priority for you regarding your child, step-child or romantic partner can be a confounding and absolute "*No*" for the other party—and they're not going to budge. When we act from a sense of emotional authority, our strong feelings make it easy to discount the other person's concerns in favor of our own. Our agenda is *superior* since it's based on love and fierce attachment. We couldn't let go of our emotional authority even if we tried, nor would we want to. In the example above, both stepmom and mom were likely experiencing a strong sense of emotional jurisdiction because their actions came from love and concern for the child.

This dynamic sets us up for clashes of the worst kind, since it is rooted in either maternal instincts of protection—or romantic attachments to the person we have chosen as our mate. Figuring out how to "work with" the other side is confusing and emotionally charged because taking a step back feels like betraying our loved ones and *abdicating our responsibilities to them.*

IN THE WORDS OF OUR READERS

Kim B. (stepmom): *"The things that make me happiest (how happy we are together, getting married, trying for a baby) are also the things that the mom, and to a lesser extent, my older stepson, dread the most. It's a struggle trying to balance feeling happy and being open about it, and taking everyone else's feelings into account. I understand why, but it does make me very sad, for everyone involved."*

K.F. (mom, stepmom): *"We have two sub-families in our house: my husband and stepson, and my son and me. After 11 years together, that line hasn't blended. It's not a huge issue, except that both of us tend to protect and support our own kid when there are issues between them. We know we're doing it, but it's hard to stop."*

Leila (stepmom): *"In the beginning, I always aligned with my husband's wishes, but as the children have gotten older, I factor in much more what they want. For instance, last year before back-to-school night for my stepson, there was a significant amount of discussion amongst the adults about whether I should attend, with both parties posturing that they knew what my stepson wanted. I happened to be picking him up from school that day and had a heart to heart with him in the car where he expressed some very complex and varied emotions. He also expressed both parent's opinions as his own, using the exact wording that I had heard* *from both of them. He and I made the decision together that I would not go—instead we would go out to a fun dinner together and 'avoid the drama.'"*

Pamela M. (divorced mom, stepmom): *"For me this resonates on many levels. We deal with three physical households, with all the kids having long-distance relationships with their dads. There's my home with my son who lives here. My ex-husband's home, where my boys go. And my husband's ex-wife, where his son and daughter live. On top of that, for several years we had a situation when my hubby was out of town all week, every week. That meant I often was a single parent Monday through Friday, then one weekend it was just me and my husband, and the next it was me, him and my kids. I really led different lives based upon who was where. Add in his kids coming to visit a few times a year and the dynamic changed again. It is like holding multiple roles and having to change on the fly. And if it is stressful for me as an adult, I can't imagine the challenge to the kids."*

JOURNAL QUESTIONS:
THREE EMOTIONAL GIVENS

For each person, name three concise emotional givens or *rights* you assume are "yours," based on a sense of emotional authority (whether the other household agrees with you or not). Examples could be from the most mundane, such as, "Only I'm allowed to take my daughter for haircuts," to the most volatile, "I live with these kids half of the time, so I have every right to participate in family therapy sessions!"

_____

_____

Extra Credit: Look at each of the statements above. To what extent would the other woman agree or disagree with you? What do you think some of her "givens" are, even if you strongly disagree with them?

_____

_____

SITUATIONS IN WHICH YOU'RE LIKELY TO BE TRIGGERED

Most of us like to imagine we're capable of meeting life's curve balls with competence and grace. But here are the zingers that will likely trip up even the most placid Buddhist. Place a checkmark next to the most common triggers that set off *your* instinctual alarms.

UNWANTED COMMUNICATION

This ranges from true emergencies, like a trip to the ER, to poor excuses to "connect," such as contacting the other parent to remind them that their child needs to brush their teeth at night.

> **Holly O. (divorced mom, stepmom)**: *"My biggest trigger is what 'gets back to me' through family and mutual friends about how I am somehow failing the kids because of the differences in political and religious ideology between our households, and the insinuation that I am pushing my son to go in the military because his stepdad is active duty. The worst is when the kids (both teens) try to talk to their dad about their feelings, only to be asked, "Is that how you feel—or is that how Mom tells you to feel?" I'm a big girl, I've learned to handle the criticism. It's more about involving the kids and doubting them that makes me see red."*

> **Crystal B. (stepmom)**: *"My husband's ex-wife would text him over twenty times a day. They rarely pertained to the kids. They mainly consisted of complaints about him as a father or me as a stepmother. Even though he eventually learned to ignore them and turn his phone off, they were extremely intrusive. Not only would they interrupt our family and alone time, but sometimes he'd be in such a bad mood after reading them that the rest of our evening would be ruined."*

MONEY

This ranges from child support, alimony, and after-school activities, to newborn "ours" babies and the future you want for your children. Single moms may see the other household with two incomes and believe it's unjust, while stepmoms may see a good percentage of her husband's income going toward supporting his ex-wife.

> **J.M. (stepmom)**: *"Last year, the boys were regularly sent to school without food packed or money to buy lunch. We were constantly getting bills from the school that they fed them and money was owed. This year is only a week and a half in, and on Friday my stepson called me from school. He had no food and no money to buy it and wanted me to do something. Much as I try to see her side and get my husband to as well, in this I can't think of any justification. Everything else, I can see how it's probably just something we see differently. Not providing lunch? I don't get it."*

> **Heather G. (divorced mom)**: *"I used to get triggered when I would think about my ex-husband being behind on child support, but then has a new house built or goes on a ski vacation. I guess as much as it has annoyed me in the past, I can't change it, so I don't focus on it. I handle what I can control and give the rest to God."*

BREACHED PRIVACY

This ranges from feeling unsafe, like you're being watched and judged in your own home, one house grilling the kids about what goes on at the other house or perhaps having private information make its way to the other household without your permission.

> **Leila (stepmom)**: *"Our biggest trigger is any time I, as the stepmom, do anything for the kids publicly. I have to do my good deeds on the sly or make sure only my husband gets the 'credit.'"*

Alissa (divorced mom): *"The worst feeling in the world was getting my reputation pulled through the mud and my parenting put under a microscope in order to win a court battle. Then a year later, my ex-husband states he never wanted half the things they fought for."*

ATTACKING YOUR PUBLIC REPUTATION

Any of this sound familiar? Having outright lies or dirty laundry aired on a blog or social networking page with passive-aggressive Facebook statuses or tweets. Your employer is contacted with false accusations in an attempt to get you fired. Word leaks back to you from former friends about something you supposedly did or said that is patently false.

M.E. (stepmom): *"Where to start? Her telling the skids that she can't buy them _____ (fill in the blank) because daddy doesn't pay enough; the allegations of abuse and neglect submitted to court; hearing from the stepkids that, "Mom doesn't like you," the horrible emails attacking my marriage, and the refusal to follow the court order all infuriate me."*

Jessica M. (divorced mom): *"The latest is seeing my son come to me with his Facebook account, asking why his dad said I kidnapped him (I just picked him up after normal visitation) and that his mother should be burned at the stake like witches used to be."*

HURTFUL, AGGRESSIVE BEHAVIOR

This could be anything from making a public scene, such as yanking the child away from the other parent or stepparent when it's not their parenting time to being yelled at during a school event.

S. B. (divorced mom): *"In my case, I felt it was her insistence on being 'the other mom' right away. She kept referring to the kids* *as 'ours' (mine and hers) and how we were going to raise them. I really think if she would have backed off and let me get to know her and start to feel comfortable with her, then she and I might have at least become friendly."*

Legal Issues

One parent may repeatedly threaten the other with legal action or consistently violate the custody order. From using the law to refuse a stepparent access to important medical information, to making unilateral decisions when the custody agreement clearly states both parents must be in agreement.

> **K.K. (divorced mom, stepmom):** *"The mom disregarding the court order is like a red rag to a bull to me. It literally can get me from calm to enraged in less than 60 seconds. This can be custody stuff, withholding the stepkids, organising things during my partner's time, not sticking to transportation orders and especially guardianship issues, where she completely cuts my partner out of any information or decision making."*

Control And Power

This could range from dictating how the other house should parent to telling the stepmom or mom what she can and can't do. Other examples are being late for pick-ups and meetings, and scheduling conflicts, especially ones that ruin your plans and are accompanied by a "But I already told you about this!"

> **Dora P. (stepmom, mom):** *"Like her saying it is none of my husband's business where his kids are when she's gone and then she leaves them somewhere else. But then if he goes to work a few hours early, she demands to know where the kids are and if they are with me, that they be sent home immediately."*

WHAT'S "BEST" FOR THE KIDS

It's easy for all of us to assume we're right with this one! This may entail trying to force your values on the other household or questioning them when they make parenting decisions you don't agree with.

> **Christine O. (stepmom):** *"I help my stepson with his homework because I'm often home with him. I'm not a fan of the word 'never,' so this is big for me to say, but to my knowledge, my stepson's homework has* never *gotten done at his mother's. I struggle with not judging her for that, especially because my stepson is a very intelligent kid with great potential. If she sees me doing school-related things with him, it doesn't go over well. It is hard for me to balance her feelings and feeling like if I don't help, my stepson could miss out."*

> **J.B. (divorced mom):** *"My ex-husband is extremely cheap and it always feels triggery-y when I can hear the judgments oozing from him at every turn. One of my latest favorites: my boy had a stomach bug and had an accident while we were out. I helped him clean himself up (he is seven) but his underwear was annihilated, so I tossed them. Later on Facetime, my son mentioned to my ex-husband that he got sick and 'Mom had to throw away my underwear." Instead of just letting it go, my ex-husband had to sarcastically say 'Well, to some people, money grows on trees so they choose to just waste things, instead of putting them in bags to wash.' I don't care that we have different money attitudes, but I do care that he feels the need to judge me in front of our children. This has been going on the whole time I've known him."*

FEELING EXCLUDED AND HELPLESS

Stepkids may come over and completely ignore the stepmom, such as only offering to get their dad something from the kitchen when the stepmom is sitting right next to him. If the mom isn't repartnered, she may feel like a "loser" at public functions where her ex-husband, the stepmom and the children are present, appearing as a family.

> **Leila (stepmom)**: "*What triggers me: When their mom assumes she always gets the final say and that she is the* primary *decision maker for the kids, over my husband. She does this a lot. We have gotten better managing it emotionally over the years by just letting it go, mostly.*"

OLD BAGGAGE

Current situations can be extra painful and difficult to deal with if we haven't processed the past and healed sore spots. Whereas you'd normally be able to cope and move on, it totally throws you for a loop.

> **Zen (divorced mom, former stepmom)**: "*In my case, the other woman is literally the woman my ex left me for, so it's even more painful to have her presence waved in my face. Last night when I picked my daughter up, they had set up a row of chairs in the front yard with a few friends to sit and await my pick up. It was like being on display as part of their party entertainment line-up. This has happened several times. Before, I rarely made an appearance when the ex-wife picked up my stepdaughter. I just knew that wasn't cool, especially as time went on and she became more uncomfortable with my being a part of her daughter's life.*"

If you found yourself nodding your head and checking off each item, don't despair. In the rest of this book, you're going to learn how to calm yourself in those intense, anxiety-ridden moments—or better yet, avoid them altogether.

AS WE LEAVE THIS CHAPTER

Can you see now how anyone in these dual-family situations is likely to run up against not one or two simple problems, but several loaded ones—through no fault of their own? The good news: you're not crazy or emotionally inept. You aren't a failure for finding these issues so difficult. And you're *certainly* not alone.

If many of your struggles are actually to be expected, then it's important to start building the strongest support network you can. No one should have to take this confusing journey by themselves. Having friends and family you can turn to will help you transform this challenge into one where you thrive, hopeful and empowered.

That said, not all support is created equal. Some well-meaning advice will hold you back and keep you stuck. Some could even make your situation worse! In the next chapter, we'll get you started thinking about how to create the most kick-ass group of friends and comrades possible.

CHAPTER 2

SUPPORT: ARE YOU AND YOUR FRIENDS ACTUALLY MAKING IT WORSE?
(validation from others vs. your own higher wisdom)

BUT I'M TRYING SO HARD!

We seek out help for conflict with the other woman because it's so confusing and pervasive. But are you really getting the support you *need*—or just the kind you *want*? They're not always the same thing.

When was the last time you took part in a huge bitch session? Perhaps on Facebook or with a group of friends where you purged all your pent-up emotions? Immediately afterward you probably felt lighter. But how about later on in the day? Were you more at peace or angrier and more hurt than before you began venting?

Our goal in this chapter isn't to determine who's right or wrong in your situation. It's to discern between good and bad advice and to shine a light on your behaviors that are contributing to the problem (though you may not realize it and would vigorously argue otherwise).

An honest, effective support system is necessary to achieve progress with your mom/stepmom dissension—one that gets you someplace that's actually *good for you*. Whether the other woman is just stubborn and cantankerous or an actual psychopath, if you don't own your own ego-based stuff here, your situation will never get better. And trust us—we *all* have it to own.

IN JENNIFER'S WORDS

Once, one of my best friends told me I was being too self-absorbed, spending all my time on my own problems and not enough time listening to my friends. My face grew hot and I sputtered on the phone with her, mumbling something about being sorry, trying to do better. I burst into tears after I hung up. Then my tears flared into anger.

I hauled out some paper to sort through what I'd just heard. My first inclination was to think "How dare she? Life has been really hard lately. If I can't confide in friends, then who *can* I talk to? What a lot of nerve! Maybe she's not such a good friend after all!" For a brief moment, I shocked myself, considering letting our friendship die off from attrition. And then I wondered if there could be any truth to what she had said, however bluntly.

If I was honest, I *had* been pretty clueless about the inner lives of my friends. Overwhelmed, stressed, and hugely ashamed, I was having a hard time making ends meet. My migraines were off the charts. Seemingly stuck between a rock and a hard place, I felt weirdly justified in ignoring my friendships, even testing them, perversely wondering if they could withstand long stretches of neglect.

My dear, blunt friend had given me a gift, painful though it was. She was a rare bird who would call it as she saw it. If you disagreed, she was open to hearing why, but she didn't mince words. She'd stuck her neck out and there was good reason to pay attention. I had initially promised to do better with her after feeling attacked, but now I really *meant* it.

IN JENNA'S WORDS

Once, my husband, his ex-wife, and I attended an all-weekend parenting class. The ex-wife and I had made some progress by that time, so I expected the weekend to be somewhat easy. The vibe of the class was pretty hippy-dippy, with lots of love, bonding and hugging. Not exactly comfy for me. At one point, the instructor said, "*Even when you're divorced, you're* still *married to the other person.*" Ouch. My husband and I saw it differently.

As the class progressed, I started to feel nervous, clinging to my husband more than I normally would in the ex's presence. Tingling in my fingers turned into a knot in my stomach. My anger at her for her past behavior started to mount. The uneasiness increased. I wanted the weekend to be over, but was too proud to admit it to myself, much less my husband—especially because she hadn't done anything that weekend to warrant my feelings. She was friendly and polite and, on the surface, all was good.

The more the instructors tried to bond the parents together, the more I tried insert myself into the equation, to show her *"I'm here!"* At the same time, I was whispering to myself, "Jenna, chill out! What's gotten into you? You're acting like a jealous schoolgirl!"

It seemed like the workshop would never end. If I had to see my husband and his ex-wife hug one more time, I was going to scream, or at least fake some acute illness. Finally, the weekend was over and I could breathe again. Unfortunately, it didn't end before I did some real damage to my relationship with my husband's ex.

We advocate owning your own shit, so here's mine.

The first thing I did that I'm not proud of was act overly demonstrative with my husband. I'm a very affectionate person, but typically I hold back in her presence. Now, it was more than just affection, I was *glued* to him. I no longer cared to modify my behavior for someone who I felt didn't deserve my kindness.

The second thing I did was the clincher that threw her over the edge. If we had any chance of a decent relationship before, it was probably out the window after this. Any time the instructors talked about a parent's potentially negative behavior and it was something my husband and I believed we had experienced with her, I would make eye contact with him. I'd glance his way and we'd both know I was thinking: *Remember that?*

Unbeknownst to me, she saw this. I imagine she thought I was laughing at her, but it was my way of reconnecting with my husband when I felt extremely vulnerable. I wasn't being malicious, I just felt unnerved, threatened. I later found out that my actions angered and hurt her so deeply that she'd never forgive me for it.

One of the most anguishing aspects of this experience was the fact that my husband agreed; I had acted inappropriately. He said he'd cringed a little whenever I'd looked at him because he knew she could see it. Wait—what? My own husband thought I was behaving badly? But he's *always* on my side! His words were a stake in my heart. My husband is the most honest person I've ever met and it's one of the things I love most about him. To be on the receiving end of that honesty was painful and admittedly served as a good wake-up call.

In the months that followed, every time I thought back on that parenting weekend *I felt ill* and couldn't figure out *why.* I didn't even like mentioning the name of the instructors or the organization because every time I did I felt shame that I'd behaved so badly and felt so insecure. It wasn't like me. It wasn't until I was actually writing this story that I came to fully understand where my feelings stemmed from and why I behaved the way I did.

THE BLIND LEADING THE BLIND

Traditionally, we're looking for three main components when we seek help for our problems: sympathy, understanding and agreement. But each of these elements is a double-edged sword. They can help and heal—or lead us down a self-defeating road.

Here are the *seemingly* positive aspects of support:

SYMPATHY

Friends and family members are rooting for you. They are on *your* team. If someone has wronged you, your listener is pissed off on your behalf. If you're hurt, they're concerned. If you're scared, they reassure.

UNDERSTANDING AND FAMILIARITY

Friends and family *get* it. They know all the players involved, the backstory, and most of the relevant details. You can speak in "shorthand" and they instantly understand what's at stake and the options you're considering.

AGREEMENT

Friends and family echo your own words back to you, aghast at the stupidity, insensitivity or evil intentions of the other person. They bolster your sense of feeling rightfully hurt or angry as you vow to take action, show the other side how it's done, or that you're the "better person." In many ways, "the other side" is automatically the villain, no matter what their motives, fears or concerns are.

QUIZ—RATE YOUR DIFFERENT SOURCES OF VALIDATION

How are your current attempts to solve your most pressing problems working?

Think of specific friends and family, co-workers, and websites or online forums where you are an active participant or reader. Mark an X in the column that best describes how you feel after receiving support from that person or group.

	Validated, I have new ideas that make me feel empowered and hopeful	Validated, like someone gets it – and that's all I need right now	Validated, but feel worse – angrier and more victimized than ever	Invalidated – not understood, all alone and more hopeless than ever
Family				
Friends				
Co-workers				
Online support (list each site on a separate line)				

Any surprises? What did you discover as you thought about this issue more deeply?

_____

_____

_____

In The Words Of Our Readers

> **Annie (stepmom):** "*My biggest problem with many stepmom 'support' groups: suddenly my little problem grows as everyone else dumps their own issues onto mine. When I stopped venting to*

people and just dealt with the issues privately instead, there was a lot less stress, a lot fewer voices in my head. I was able to deal with the mom and only the mom, not the ghosts of the other 'evil moms' as well."

Holly O. (divorced mom): *"I have many people in my life all too willing to validate me when I rant about my child's stepmom. I had never lashed out at her, after many years of dealing with each other. Finally, the last time we argued (after being validated by a friend), I said those mean and hateful words you should probably never say to someone who has shared in the raising of your kids: 'Because I'm their* mother!*' I shouted it. It was hurtful, no matter how much she pushed me or asked for it. To me, I crossed the line. It's been over a year since we last spoke and I wish I could take it back."*

Katie P. (stepmom): *"I had a co-worker that would help me write my emails to the mom. We were so worked up that we took any* response *from her poorly. I reread a lot of those emails after the mom and I started to get along and realized I misread or misinterpreted a lot of what she wrote, because I was so wrapped up in how much I disliked her. My husband and I would do the same thing with his correspondence too. It's important to remember people love other people's drama! There are way more escalators than diffusers in this world."*

K.K. (mom, stepmom): *"Talking to people who won't call you on your part in things and only see things from a similar perspective is not helpful. I found the more I moaned about my stepchild's mom, the angrier and more unhappy I got, to the point that I lost myself in it all."*

HOW WE SET THE STAGE FOR INEFFECTIVE SUPPORT

We hear plenty of stepmoms and divorced moms say, "I thought I was *the only one* struggling with these feelings." If there are millions of women suffering with these issues, it doesn't make sense for so many of us to feel so alone. Is it possible our fears are helping us perpetuate the wrong *kind* of support? We inadvertently practice some very common behaviors that don't really help us in the long run. We:

- **Hide or isolate when it's really hard**: You withdraw from friends and family to lick your wounds in private. Maybe if you don't talk about it, it will all just go away? Or perhaps saying the words out loud makes your problems all too real and painful. Asking for help is a last resort or not an option at all. You know your behavior is unhealthy, but you're used to crumbling in isolation and don't show this side of yourself to even your closest friends.

- **Continually ask for help but don't make any changes**: You're good at asking for support, but you also feel chagrined because you're repeating yourself when you relay the same old feelings and complaints. You suspect you're making yet one more pass on the merry-go-round of conflict and chaos, but honestly, the idea of implementing all the helpful suggestions that people come up with just seems overwhelming. You don't know where to start, so you… don't.

- **Feel pressured to seem more put-together than you actually feel**: Society expects women to be the multi-taskers of the world, the emotional "managers" of the family. Other women have mastered their divorced families and stepfamilies, so why are *you* having such trouble? What does it *mean* about you? You might want to prove that you can be a "super" stepmom, but when the honeymoon is over and everyone's personalities are clashing, not having your home life gel into a loving family can make you feel like a failure. Divorced moms often share in that same feeling of shame as a woman. If a mother "failed" her primary responsibility (her children) and cannot even provide a foundation of security and stability for her children's future, then how can she feel good about *anything* as a mother going forward?

Can you relate? What are some experiences in your past where you sought unhealthy support?

_____

_____

Did you ever seek help and have it go surprisingly well? What was the difference?

_____

_____

THE CONSEQUENCES OF AGREEMENT-ONLY SUPPORT

One component of lousy support, agreement, can get us into real trouble. If you have your own team of Yes Men and Women, nodding their heads as you explain your tale of woe, you're potentially missing out on one of the most valuable perspectives of all. It may be the answer to your problems—*but it's also one you can't see*—which is why you're in this situation in the first place! Trouble is that your listener can't see that fresh perspective either.

Most advice is not objective. It's created by each person's personal opinions, shortcomings, unconscious beliefs and old baggage. They're likely projecting previous negative experiences onto your situation, which can be really bad for helping you create nuanced, complex insights. If you and your friends don't understand important elements of your situation, then for that very reason, their advice is incomplete and potentially harmful, sending you off in the wrong direction.

What you don't know *can* hurt you. Think back to the dark ages, when we didn't understand basic correlations that we all take for granted now: how germs are the reason for infection, how everyone thought sailors would fall off the edge of the ocean into outer space, that smoking and sun exposure can cause cancer.

Is it *really* such a dramatic catastrophe if you indulge in a little comfort now and then? You decide. Here are the cut-and-dried consequences of seeking agreement-only support:

- **No new information:** Instead of opening your mind to other ideas and actions that might actually *resolve* the conflict, you're now stuck *reinforcing* your current way of thinking and patterns of behavior.

- **You back yourself into a corner:** Rather than deal with the mess and ambiguity of reality, where you admit your mistakes and make amends, you feel compelled to stick to your black-and-white story with no shades of grey. Friends and family expect this as well.
- **Keeps you accountability-free:** On the surface, it seems like a good idea to blame others. We remain the victim, always in the right, while others play the villain. This sympathy loop keeps you powerless and continually upset since you must generate new problems to keep a constant supply of commiseration.
- **People get tired of all the repetition:** The only people who like to hear others complain without taking steps to fix the problem are people who are just as miserable. If you've ever thought "What has become of me? I never used to be this negative. *I'm* even a little sick of me!" then it's time to change your tune.
- **Encourages you to distort the truth:** There's a good chance you're not telling the whole story when you're working from the Land of Heightened Emotions. This is a nice way of saying you may be (*cough*) exaggerating (*cough*) the facts, or conveniently leaving a few important details out. Like the consequences listed above, this shrinks your available options. You also have to consistently stick to a particular "version" of events, which can be hard to remember!

IN THE WORDS OF OUR READERS

Brynn (divorced mom, stepmom): *"I was being a brat. I was judging their relationship (ex-husband/stepmom) and being connected at the hip, but it's really none of my business. I wasn't being put in my place before. It took a bold honesty to start down a different path, because the one I was on? Wasn't cutting it."*

Aimee G. (stepmom): *"I have learned from my own stupidity that no matter how many high fives I got from my friends, it is not very wise to vent to all on Facebook. Who knew? One day after a lot of angry emails and phone calls between my husband and his ex, she decided to update her status with 'Karma is going to come*

*back and bite you in the ass!' My response, also on Facebook, was
'Karma is going to come back and bite you in your HUGE ass!'
I know, I know... not one of my finest moments. All my friends
laughed and said, 'Way to go, Aimee!' It may have given me the
attention I needed at the time, but I am not laughing about it
anymore.*

*That one sentence, those thirteen words, caused such havoc that will
never really be repaired. It ruined my relationship with the boys.
It made my husband's life difficult when dealing with his ex. No
matter how many times I have apologized or how many years in
the past it was, my stepchildren's mom will never truly forgive me.
It was such a petty thing to do and I am not that kind of person.
Every time that mistake comes back to haunt me I feel like such
an ugly person, and rightfully so, because that was a horrendous
thing to do!"*

HOW TO TELL IF YOU MIGHT BE LYING TO YOURSELF

There's a funny thing that happens when we feel a very strong emotion. Not
only are we sure of the *feeling* cascading through our systems, but we are also
intensely sure of the *facts* (which are biased in our favor). Ever been dead-set
on your interpretation of a situation, only to make a 180-degree shift in your
perspective later? Same principle at work here. We lie to ourselves and distort
the truth to justify ourselves after the fact.

More accurately, we first evoke our negative emotions *by the thoughts we
think*. Beliefs and opinions pop into our minds and microseconds later, almost
instantaneously, the feelings follow. The factual "proof" for our beliefs then
becomes the *strength* of our emotions. Irrational, but beautifully convenient,
wouldn't you say?

No one wants to believe this formula applies to them, but our thoughts are
often wildly inaccurate since they're based on subconscious patterns we absorbed,
without question, as children. Our mental habits play themselves out, but while
this is happening, we have the niggling sense that we're not being entirely honest—with others or ourselves. When we're tearing the other woman apart to
family and friends, we might also be thinking, "Hmm, I did that very thing just
a few months ago, but *this* is different! Right?" To escape our discomfort, we fall

back on little tricks of the ego, taking comfort in feeling superior, in "showing her up." We bask in eager agreement from our friends. We'll even relish the cozy role of the victim, the one who's obviously suffered the most. However, there are always many sides to every story:

> *There are the things you can see clearly, but she can't.*
> *There are things she can see clearly, but you can't.*
> *There are things you can't see because of old patterns, but everyone else can.*
> *There are things she can't see because of old patterns, but everyone else can.*

Same thing for all the other players involved!

Numerous studies on memory recall prove that what we *think* we remember about a situation is highly subjective. If you read *No One's the Bitch*, you may recall that Jennifer and Carol both had completely different recollections about their very first encounter. Jennifer met Carol when she rode up on a motorcycle with her ex-husband, David. Carol first met Jennifer in a car when her youngest stepdaughter forced her to get out and say hello. Who was right? They still don't know to this day!

Just because you feel or believe something doesn't make it true.

QUIZ—OOPS, I GUESS I DID IT AGAIN

We can't always tell when we've got the horse blinders on, but it's worth examining your previous behavior to see how you might react to future challenges. In the middle of a difficult situation, do you find yourself (put a check next to each item that applies):

- Repeating the most inflammatory parts of the story to a number of people?
- Ruminating and repeatedly worrying about the what-ifs?
- Trying to convince yourself you're in the right?
- Worrying that you may be overlooking some important, but conflicting details?
- Leaving out any parts of your story where you may be to blame?

- Playing out revenge fantasies where you come out the winner and she's publicly humiliated?
- Assuming you're clearly miles ahead of her in terms of intelligence and accomplishment?
- Struggling, once again, with friends, a partner or co-workers? Does it seem like *someone* is always doing something to set you off?

SCORING GUIDE:

For each item that you checked, give yourself five points.

0-5 points: *Do you live in a nunnery? We're thinking you're very familiar with Yoda or deep, but totally confusing Zen parables, because you rock.*

10-20 points: *You're wonderfully human. We find ourselves pissy and judgmental too sometimes. As long as you know you're doing it and are consistently shooting for more…*

25-40 points: *Gah! It's hard feeling this way, isn't it? (We know. Been there, done that.) The good news is that not only are you angry at her, you're probably pretty angry at yourself too. Forgiving yourself is a great way to start alleviating some of the stress—and she doesn't have to do one thing differently for you to gain some relief.*

How'd you score? What do you think of your results?

SHE'S THE HERO OF HER STORY TOO

Many problems between houses start because someone is actually *just trying to solve a problem.* A father desperately misses his kids. A stepmom is trying to feel a sense of belonging in a family with lots of history that came before her. A mom feels resentful including the stepmom in decisions that used to be between her and the kids' father. People struggle with their emotions and act in less-than-helpful ways that normally don't "apply" to them. And yet it does—*when they're in pain.*

We excuse our actions because *we know* what's at stake for us. We forgive our own bad behavior. We rationalize it because we understand our own secret motivations. But what about the other side? *Where does your compassion for them begin and end?* Can you see their pain? Is it possible to reinterpret their manipulative, crazy conduct?

If you find yourself swinging back and forth on the pendulum of being a hero or martyr in your situation, consider whether your empathy is too one-sided. Have you ever considered the possibility that *you* might be causing just as much havoc in the other woman's life as she is in yours? Even though her bad judgment is clear as day to you, chances are she's also surrounded by friends and family who see her as being in the right, *just like you.* Weird, huh?

IN THE WORDS OF OUR READERS

K.K. (divorced mom, stepmom): *"Last week was one of the worst weeks I can remember. After months of court proceedings, an order was made, and the mom decided she would simply not follow it. I was so angry I made myself physically ill with stress. It just seemed like there was no way to protect these kids. I had to face my ugliest self, and the more I talked about it, the worse it got. She became some inhuman monster in my head, for whom I couldn't feel anything but contempt. That is so outside of who I generally am. I'm the reasonable one, the empathetic one, the one who always gives the benefit of the doubt, and suddenly, I was unable to do that. It was hard to decide who I hated more, me or the mom.*
It would have been really helpful if people around me had said more forcefully, 'Hey, this is so not you,' earlier on when I started getting so angry a few months ago. I think I have learned that a problem shared can become a problem doubled! I'm coming to a better place with it all now, and catch myself when I am about to start a tirade about the mom."

K. F. (divorced mom, stepmom): *"I had an 'aha' moment about this recently. I'm a divorced mom and stepmom, but I primarily identify with stepmoms because that journey has been so much* *harder for me. I used to think: I never asked for this, I never wanted this. As a child, I never dreamed of being a stepmom or raising someone else's kids.*

And then, one day I realized that the mom probably had similar thoughts and was thinking: I never dreamed of this, I never asked for this, I never wanted to be a divorced mom, I never wanted another woman to raise my kids.

I realized in that moment that we are two halves of the same coin. Neither of us asked for this experience. Each of us longed for something different, but our reality is what it is, and both of us need to make the best of it. To even take it a step further, both of our dreams are shattered. This isn't the life that either of us wanted. We are both adjusting and making do."

Erika (stepmom): *"This was definitely a turning point for us, with a hurt we had in common. When I reached out to the mom, she had just lost a baby. I had lost a baby four years back and it was something I never quite recovered from. In the midst of our fights, anger, and hatred, I saw a sadness in her that I knew all too well. And for me, this was the realization that the mom was no different than me. She had a heart, she hurt, she cried, she suffered through a loss that I would wish on no one. Putting everything aside, I really just wanted to hug her and I told her, 'I know your pain.' For us, that was the beginning of our new relationship. Sometimes, it takes things like this to see that we all bleed blood, we all have a heart that beats, and if I would just open up my heart to her, I would find so much more that we had in common, and that's just what I did. 'Blessings in disguise' is what I call it!"*

Both stepmoms and divorced moms experience the same emotions. Neither has more noble emotions or suffers more "purely!" But the fuel for those emotions comes from a different source that is unique to each role. *This is one reason the two women cannot understand why the other person is acting as she is.* If we were in her shoes, in her position, the behavior would seem perfectly justified.

As much as it might pain you to believe you have anything in common with the divorced mom or stepmom, it's true.

Do any of these common feelings below sound familiar? Put a checkmark next to any emotions you can especially relate to:

- *Attacked:* You're frightened and angry that someone is so rude and aggressive when you aren't even reciprocating.
- *Victimized:* No one else you know has to deal with your situation. You want everyone to know how much stress you're under.
- *Deeply Hurt:* You can't believe that anyone would *ever* behave this way to you. You feel wounded.
- *Minimized and Invalidated:* All the positive things you are trying to bring to this situation, all your hard work and sacrifice is being completely overlooked.
- *Anger:* How dare she or he act like this to you, the kids, the stepkids or your partner? It's totally wrong.
- *Powerless:* You don't know how to make it stop. You seemingly have no control over your life.
- *Sadness and Grief:* You've forgiven and tried again until you've become hopeless and depleted. If only there was a friendship there, life could be so much better.
- *Rejected and Rebuffed:* You extended an olive branch to her, but it feels like she grabbed it and swatted you over the head with it. You feel stung.
- *Territorial:* You feel like your turf is being infringed upon; there's nothing that's just *yours*. Somehow, everything is tinged or tainted by her.
- *Alone and Isolated:* There's no one around who really understands. Your lack of resources is making everything ten times harder.
- *Self-sabotaging:* You have the gnawing feeling that some of your old baggage is being activated in all the chaos, but have no idea how to fix it. You watch yourself play out old patterns and kick yourself for it later.

Remember, the *feelings* drive the behavior. *To both of you*, your behavior seems perfectly normal, given the emotion roiling beneath it.

AS WE LEAVE THIS CHAPTER

The kind of help you invite into your life can make the difference between staying stuck and unhappy—or creating new insights that blast you forward into healing. Which one will you seek even if it involves discomfort at times? The wisdom and advice that is reflected back to you creates different possibilities, like alternate paths stretching out into the future. Choose wisely!

In Section Three on *Support,* we'll show you how to leave behind the elements of your support system that aren't working and create more effective ones.

Ready to switch gears for a while? Good. The next chapter was written by Jenna's husband and it's for the men, but we know you're going to read it too. We did!

CHAPTER 3

MEN: WHAT DOES THE MAN IN THE MIDDLE THINK?

(conflicting loyalties vs. clear priorities)

By Mario Korf

Note: *This chapter is written by a dad, for dads. Moms and stepmoms will probably read it (because you just have to know what we're thinking), but it's not for you.*

I know how difficult it is to crack this first paragraph. It's likely you're handling your shit and there's enough on your plate without having to read a chapter in some self-help book. I understand and I'll keep it short.

I'm going to make some generalizations based on a limited sample size, skewed by my personal perceptions. I guess this is my lame attempt at a disclaimer, and if what I describe doesn't suit you, then it doesn't.

Maybe you don't have a problem being in the middle between two feisty broads, and you've figured out how to co-parent with your ex, and everyone is happy in your complex family unit. That's great, man, and I'm happy for you, but that's not my experience. I reckon this chapter speaks to the average divorced and remarried dad, and there are men on either side of that curve that I'm not reaching at all. So if you're the average dad and you're still with me, I'll share my story and hope that some of it resonates with you.

I'm not a therapist and I'm not trying to be your life coach. I've made mistakes and learned a thing or two from them. I might slip in the occasional word of advice, or a cautionary note, but I'm certainly not going to lay a bunch of "shoulds" on you or tell you what to do.

HORSES AND ZOMBIES

I was at the dinner table one day, briefing Jenna and my teenage boys about my plan for the Zombie Apocalypse. My scheme involved horses rather than a car, which we would ride to a large boat stocked with provisions (because zombies don't swim, right?) We all laughed and contributed to the ridiculous plan, and dinner went by with smiles. The next day, I got an irate phone call and emails from my ex saying that I must include her in these stories. She was livid I didn't rescue her as well. Never mind that I can't ride a horse, and that zombies don't exist. According to her, I had traumatized the kids by leaving their mother out of the story. Apparently, this was the equivalent to having her brains eaten by the dead.

I usually wad up this kind of behavior and throw it away, but it got me thinking. Did I traumatize the kids? Had I done something wrong? It took me a minute or two before I figured out the problem; she still thinks it's my duty to provide for and protect her. Somehow the ten-year span that included separation, divorce, dating, living with another woman, and then marrying her, became trivial details.

And that's women for you. I can't figure it out, but I understand that women see a bigger picture that encompasses *all* things, not just rational things. Some women more than others. If you've ever had a woman mad at you all day for something that happened to her in a dream, you know what I'm talking about.

PROVIDE AND PROTECT

However you feel about it, women understand that it's a man's role to provide and protect. It's why rich old geezers and brainless thugs have arm candy that'll have you shaking your head in disbelief. And it's why you'll probably do or have done things for your ex that your wife feels like you shouldn't be doing. Maybe you extended an invitation to a family event, tried to include her in a birthday party for the kids, didn't charge her for something you paid for, or made some other kind of effort to help her out.

My ex and I did a lot of hurtful things to each other over the years, and my friends would be surprised to find that I still do the occasional supportive thing for her. She typically doesn't know about them, but I do it anyway. For example, I remind my sons to get her flowers on Valentine's Day; I don't nickel and dime her on the shared finances; I've rearranged my summer vacation plans around her (sometimes fickle) plans. Jenna asked me about this: how could I feel any charity toward someone who I've shared such a bitter and dysfunctional relationship with? Sometimes I wonder that myself, but I reckon it's because a man's instinct is to provide and protect, and this extends to everyone. Even the ones who hurt you.

Providing for and protecting your ex can send mixed signals. She might wonder "Why is he helping me?" After over-analyzing that for too long, who knows what she might come to believe about you. Or about you and her. So if you can make that decision to completely separate yourselves, maybe you're ahead of the game. I don't know, I can't help helping others, and I'm sure I've sent my share of confusing messages to, well, both women.

What *isn't* confusing is that I will provide and protect for my wife above all others. Part of that is never letting my ex speak badly about her. If my ex says something even remotely negative about Jenna, I immediately let her know that's not okay, and I will not be communicating with her if she continues. Setting a firm boundary reinforces that there isn't a you-and-her anymore. If you let your ex say something negative, she might get the idea that she's colluding with you. Sending the message that it's over and that there is no longer any "sacred bond" is important.

Just as I wouldn't let my ex say anything negative about my wife, neither would I let my kids disrespect her. Ever. If the kids disrespect her, they disrespect me. This is a message from me to the kids, not from her.

FIXING THINGS

Men like to fix things, especially the easy and obvious problems in day-to-day life. A sticking doorjamb or leaky faucet is our bread and butter, so when the women in our life start arguing, we tend to want to fix that as well.

And why not? Why should a simple misunderstanding between two grown women be any harder to fix than an item on a honey-do list? I don't know, but it's on the order of nuclear physics to untangle the web of a simple *she-said-she-said* between two women you married. Before making that mistake, realize that whatever perfectly logical middle ground you inhabit will be considered "taking *her* side" by *both* of them. My advice is to always take your wife's side, even if she's wrong (especially if she's wrong). It will not work the other way around.

Anyway, they'll figure it out eventually. Or not. But it ain't your problem. The world would be a better place if we all just got along, but from my personal experience, it doesn't always work out that way.

Another thing that might not be worth fixing is anything in your ex-wife's house. Fixing a contraption that only you understand is a baited trap. A light bulb she can't reach is certainly easier, but may not be a good idea. Of course it depends on your relationship with your ex—these warnings are meaningless if everyone gets along, but if you have a high-conflict relationship, the list of things you can fix is short. I've learned to keep it all in my house.

When it comes to fixing things in a more general sense, your wife isn't going to understand some of the things you have to do. Oh man, this is going to get me in hot water, but there are things a man needs to do that his wife just doesn't need to be involved in. These are not bad things, mind you, or untrustworthy things, but details that she just won't understand. Women in general love to get all up in your business. They need to know the how, what, when, where and why. But what they really mean by that is that they need to feel comforted, and that everything is going to be all right. But they mistakenly believe that knowing the details is directly related to their safety. Nope. Sometimes the opposite is closer to the truth.

You know what is best, and you certainly don't need my permission to do it. If this becomes the start of an argument, you have my sincere apology. Jenna and Jennifer will address this issue with your wife in another chapter, so don't press the issue just yet. Let's move onto the kids.

THEY AREN'T HER KIDS

Your wife probably doesn't adore it when she's sitting on the couch and your kid's stinky feet are in her face. They aren't her flesh and blood, and she doesn't have the unconditional love for them that you have. But there's a certain strength in that, because your wife married you, not your children. She's there because of you, not the kids, or possibly *in spite of* the kids.

When she started dating you, it was probably apparent early on that she came second to the kids. Maybe more often than not. And you, charmer that you are, made her fall in love with you anyway. Unless she made the mistake of dating other single dads, this might be the first relationship in which she experienced being second. That's a strange situation to be in, especially when the person is used to being number one, so it's important to keep her choice to be with you in perspective. I do this by saying the kids are my first *responsibility*, but my wife is my first *priority*. She is a wonderful person for marrying me (and dealing with my baggage), so I will put her first whenever I can.

Because your kids aren't her kids, she might feel resentful for the lack of reciprocity she gets from them. As a parent, we don't care if we give, give, and give some more to our kids and get seemingly nothing in return. We don't keep score. But day in and day out, she's cleaning their crap, making lunches, sending them out the door or picking them up at school. Or maybe she's doing less obvious things for the household, but equally important, like holding a job. What do your kids say to her for all this? How often does she get a "thank you?" How often does she get a "You're not my mom," or, "I hate you," instead?

If she feels resentful for giving all the time, that's normal. Normal people have a give-and-take relationship. Your wife needs to be reminded that her parents probably gave without reciprocity—kids behave like that. Certainly you can work on that with your kids: make sure they thank her or do things for her in return. That's part of growing up.

THEY ARE MY KIDS

Whether your wife has kids of her own or not, she probably has her own ideas about how you're raising yours. This comes largely from how she was raised, but may also come from a need to feel protected in her own environment. She can't relax with the kids going wild, or the house is too noisy or too cluttered with their things all over the place. Listen to your wife about these things without getting defensive. She may be talking about your kids and their less-than-perfect behavior, but she's not making value judgments about them. Don't take offense. Work to find a compromise.

Something I've noticed is that women in general feel that dads are too "hands-off" with the kids. From an outside perspective, I certainly fall into that group. But it's by design! I lead by example. I don't micro-manage and I give space for consequences to develop. Send a boy into the woods with nothing but a knife and he'll come out a man. Send him into the woods with everything but the kitchen sink and he comes out looking for mom. Men know this. Women, not so much.

Men who share that looser parenting style can been seen as not doing their job. Because of this, the stepmom may feel like she needs to "step in" and take on a more active parenting role. Apparently, this is a common phenomenon among stepmoms, because it often irks the moms and then everyone hears about it. The problem is that when stepmoms take on the parenting role, they do so without the one necessary requirement for the job: unconditional love. Unconditional love is why you don't need reciprocity, and it's why stinky feet in your face are cute.

But it's not that way for her, and lacking this essential requirement can get stepmoms in trouble with moms, dads and kids. In addition, moms may feel like the new wife is taking over for the dad who is "slacking off," or maybe the mom doesn't agree with the new wife's parenting style. I can't really address how moms feel about stepmoms stepping into the parenting role, but I can address how I feel. They are *my* kids.

Taking on an active parenting role is one thing, and it can be a good thing if all parties are adjusted to that. But disciplining the kids or challenging your decisions in front of them is quite another. If she does that, you need to put a stop to that for a number of reasons:

1. They are your kids, and you know best. There's no arguing this point.
2. You probably disagreed with your ex on how to raise your kids, and you divorced her. The last thing you need is two women arguing with you about how you're raising your kids.
3. You want your kids to like your wife. It's your job to protect her relationship with the kids, and to make sure they like her. Don't let her make the mistake of becoming a disciplinarian.

Now, if your wife stays out of it, but privately tells you or advises you on how you're parenting, that's great. Keep it like that by telling her how much you appreciate her advice, and how it's so smart that she doesn't step in and sully her relationship with the kids. But if she's in the opposite camp, it might be difficult to relay this message to her. Maybe if she hears it from someone else (me), that'll help.

> Stepmom: if you're guilty of disciplining your husband's kids or challenging his parenting in front of them, stop this now. Discipline isn't your job, even if he's not doing it (to your satisfaction). Whatever you think you'll accomplish isn't going to work well, and it does so at the expense of more valuable things. While the kids see you as an adult, and even as their dad's wife, you don't carry the same authority that dad and mom and do, and whatever lesson you're trying to instill won't be nearly as effective as when it comes from them. If you're thinking of examples where your discipline worked, think about what you possibly lost in the relationship in return. Is it worth casting yourself in the role of the bad guy in order to get them to pick up their socks? Really, it isn't worth it. Please stop disciplining the kids and challenging your husband's authority. It creates a rift between you and the kids, and annoys the hell out of your husband.

> What can you do? Discuss discipline with your husband and make sure it all comes from him. Don't nag him about it—that works about as well as a square wheel. If you absolutely have to do something about the dishes, the socks on the floor, or whatever it is that's getting your panties in a knot, try doing something loving and/or humorous. Eat in their room and leave the dishes on the bed. Put your clothes in their room before their friends come over. Do it with a laugh and it sends a better message.

PARALLEL PARENTING

Getting back to your ex, there comes a point where it's simply impossible to deal with each other's shit any longer. You probably both reached that point at least once already, and that's why it's over. But there are still the kids, and they need both of you. So you try again for their sake, and it works about as well as it did before. It might feel like that line from *The Godfather 3*: "Just when I thought I was out... they drag me back in."

After trying to make it work in a marriage, and then trying to co-parent outside of the marriage, I'm a strong proponent of parallel parenting. From the article "Cooperative Parenting or Parallel Parenting?" by Philip M. Stahl, Ph.D. (http://www.parentingafterdivorce.com/articles/parenting.html):

> "In this style of parenting, both of you will each learn to parent your child effectively, doing the best job each of you can do during the time you are with your child. You will continue to disengage from the other parent so that conflicts are avoided. If you determine that you cannot cooperatively parent because your level of conflict is moderate or high, disengagement and parallel parenting is the necessary style of parenting."

Professionals often recommend parallel parenting in high-conflict situations. There's less to fight about, and less for the kids to be confused about. It works. I don't know your situation, so I'm not recommending parallel parenting to you. I just wish I hadn't made it a fallback option when things got bad. It's not a last resort; it's a parenting style that should be considered from the start, especially when parents typically don't agree.

So what if your ex doesn't want to do parallel parenting? Well, that's the beauty of it—she doesn't have to! Because communication is a two-way street, only one parent needs to make the decision. Once it becomes clear that's how you're parenting, she'll fall in step. There may be a volatile adjustment period, but that's how these things go.

If you decide on parallel parenting, a few things are very important:

- Don't badmouth her or her household. You are giving up the right to discuss the way she should be doing things, so let it go.
- Do not use the kids as messengers between households.
- Support the time the kids spend with her.

- Use an integrated communication system, such as Our Family Wizard to keep track of emails, expenses, calendar, etc.

I've done parallel parenting for a couple years now and I can assure you the kids are better off for it. Not only that, but I'm happier, my wife is happier, and dammit, I think my ex is happier. Whatever fears you might have about parallel parenting are well founded, but in my experience, they didn't materialize. Children are resilient—they adapt to their surroundings and appreciate well-defined borders.

ZOMBIES AND HORSES

When I look back at that zombie story, I know I did nothing wrong, but I also know I didn't do it all right, either. If I could go back and tell the story over again, I would have included my ex, to say that she was safe or taken care of somehow. I still wouldn't have included her in my plan of horses and boats, because she's simply not part of my future. It's not rational or reasonable that I should have to do this, but it's the nice thing to do. And life's challenges (especially challenges with the ex) go easier when you're kind.

Thanks for listening, and don't tell anybody about my zombie plan. It's a secret.

CHAPTER 4
EXPECTATIONS: WHAT WERE YOU ASSUMING?
(self-control vs. controlling her)

ANYONE IN THEIR RIGHT MIND KNOWS THAT...

Expectations are what you would consider "normal" behavior. They are beliefs about how other people should behave and what should or shouldn't be happening. But that's where we run into problems. What's reasonable to you isn't necessarily sane to the other person. Earlier in Chapter 1, we discussed how we are all driven by biological imperatives that are no longer in alignment because the two family units are working against each other. Mothers and mother figures are trying to do their thing. Fathers and father figures are trying to do theirs. One marital relationship is more important to its members than the other (or the single parent, if unpartnered). Children may now have three, four or more authority figures in their lives, and each family unit expects a certain amount of loyalty, involvement and flexibility.

Every family unit has their own beliefs about:

- how to parent
- how to partner
- what is logical to expect from the other house
- how people should act after they get divorced
- how mothers or stepmothers are supposed to interact
- how husbands are supposed to be with their wives or ex-wives
- how children and stepchildren should behave

The beliefs you're acting upon are the end result of a lifetime of influences: your upbringing, your friends, school, the media, and your innate personality—even genetics. *Of course* you feel passionately about the decisions you make. *Of course* you feel as if you're doing the right thing based on the circumstances.

But so does she! Therein lies the conundrum of our dual-family relationships.

IN JENNA'S WORDS

What were my assumptions going into this? Well, since I had a stepmom growing up and never once heard her complain, and she and my mom got along well, I thought it would be a breeze! I thought we'd all be *just* fine. I'm responsible, friendly, and they had been separated for six years, so why would my husband's ex have a problem with me? Ignorantly, the thought she wouldn't like me never entered my mind.

And kids? Pffft. I never wanted my own, but his were nine and twelve and surely didn't need another mom, so I thought I was set in that department too. Needless to say, I wasn't.

Nothing was as I thought it would be. My husband's ex-wife and I clashed over things that completely perplexed me. Somehow, I kept expecting things to get better. I kept expecting her to eventually hear my words and actions as I intended them. What I've had to learn, and some days am still learning, is that as long as I'm still wishing she were different, wishing *things* were different, I'll remain frustrated. But if I can accept that she's not going to treat me the way I want to be treated, then I'm no longer disappointed. I no longer have expectations that aren't being met. And even though it's still a work in progress and it's not how I hoped it would be, I can live with that.

IN JENNIFER'S WORDS

Once I found myself up in arms over a situation in our private Facebook group (since closed) that elicited some strong feelings in me—and apparently everyone else too. The shit hit the fan when I posted a short comment about how I believed it was important for extremely young children to bond with their mothers and that equal custody between divorced parents could interfere with that process in the very early years. One of our members had a young child with medical issues and was worried about the disruption that a switch to equal custody would cause for her child.

I should have tempered my comments with some additional context, but I was trying not to violate the privacy of my ex-husband and my children. Some background: after our divorce, the kids had a hard time adjusting to going back and forth between our homes. They were four and eight and the youngest child in particular was very attached to me. Their dad and I agreed that the crying and sleeping issues were taking a toll on all of us. We decreased the number of days the kids spent with their dad—for their sake, *even though it was hard for him*. I didn't force my will upon the situation; we came up with the solution together.

But none of this information was in my original comment. It came out after a firestorm broke out over one particularly incendiary comment from a stepmom. My original response to the single mom had confirmed something the stepmom had suspected all along: our entire book and Facebook page was a ruse. What I *really* thought was that mothers were entitled to cloak manipulative, controlling behavior behind a lie: *Mothers knew best, mothers got to have the final say when it came to "their" kids. Dads were second-class citizens.* We should be ashamed of ourselves!

It would have been so easy to delete her comments and be done with it. But there were now almost 200 responses to her post. A few stepmoms agreed that we had always seemed biased and unfair toward stepmoms. They were appalled that we were siding with the moms out there bent on destroying their children's lives and the rights of their ex-husbands. Some divorced moms confessed they had always felt as if our page sided with the stepmoms, since there were so many of them. But many more women wrote back saying that it was the first time they had ever been in a group with both "sides." They had learned a lot and grown as a result.

Trying to explain the background behind my first comment, I surprised myself by sobbing at my desk for a nice, cathartic cry. Trying to mediate these kinds of altercations could be so stressful! After I elaborated, the conversation online calmed down. But I still felt upset over what this discussion had become. There was hurt, fury, and protective feelings from stepmoms for their husbands— and from moms for their children. Some women felt scorn and contempt for the other side and were proud to express it. Others did their best to give all parties the benefit of the doubt and diffuse the debate.

I *still* have to work to not judge those who approach these issues with guns blazing. Part of me expects that people *should* resolve their differences calmly and with respect, that they should be willing to consider the other person's perspective and do their best to combine it with their own. But my insistence that people behave differently is just more of the same problem.

THE RAW MATERIAL OF EXPECTATIONS

If the expectations we have in our lives are like movie scripts we're playing out, imagine all the "*shoulds*" and "*have-tos*" and "*you betters*" we're obeying at any given time. Imagine your partner's. And the children's. And hers.

If you think you don't have any unspoken dual-family rules, take a look at the following possibilities and see what springs to mind. What assumptions did you have when you first became involved in your particular situation?

Moms, what expectations did you have regarding:

- your emotional response to your ex-husband remarrying and the type of woman he would marry?
- your co-parenting relationship when he remarried?
- how your children would respond to his new wife?
- the impact your children's stepmom would have on you and your life?
- her involvement with school, doctor's appointments, other parents, etc.?

Stepmoms, what expectations did you have regarding:

- the difficulty or ease of transitioning into a stepfamily?
- what your marriage would look like?
- the level of closeness you'd feel toward your stepchildren?
- the level of acceptance you would receive from:
    * your extended family?

* your husband's extended family?
* schools, doctor's offices, other parents, etc.?
• the impact your husband's ex-wife would have on you and your life?

JOURNAL QUESTIONS:
EXPECTATIONS AND REALITY

Lots to think about, huh? Take a stroll through our readers' comments below and see if you can relate. Then come back and look again at each expectation above. Were your expectations met?

_____

_____

_____

If not, how did that expectation differ from reality? What has your reaction been to that unmet expectation? Use extra paper if you need it.

_____

_____

_____

We're not looking to solve specific problems related to your replies just yet. We simply want you to notice the way you're thinking about your situation.

IN THE WORDS OF OUR READERS

We asked our readers: what "shoulds" do you believe in? How do they differ from how the other household behaves and what actually happens?

> **Amanda D. (mom, stepmom):** *"Stepkids should have a set bedtime schedule during the week while in school. They should not stay up until 12:30 or later on a school night. They need their rest to be at their best in school, no matter their age, but especially in junior high and lower grades. At his other house, my stepson is allowed to stay up until whenever he wants to go to bed (which*

is sometimes 5 a.m. or later). This causes him to be completely exhausted when he comes home, which works against us because all he wants to do is sleep. It causes him to be lazy, which is very frustrating for me. Plus, he fights us because he's allowed to stay up until whenever at the other house and we don't do that. I know it causes resentment and frustration on everyone's part."

Heather G. (divorced mom, stepmom): *"My stepchild's mom should let my husband parent on his time as he sees fit (unless it will harm the child, and even that is subjective). When two parents separate, they lose control over what goes on in the other house. The faster they accept that, the better it is for them. I am both a divorced mom and stepmom. As a divorced mom, I do not try to exert control over the other house. They are the father's kids too!"*

Jean (stepmom): *"Each parent should be fully responsible for the children and parent their own way during their parenting time. When there is a constant need for us by the other household during their time and comparisons of households, conflict arises as it causes confusion and frustration for everyone. Respect of clear boundaries for each household is what works best for us, and aids in consistency and predictability of expectations for the children too, since the two households are so different."*

Meg (stepmom): *"I would love someone to send these questions to my stepchild's mom so I could get a clear picture of what she expects from me! Maybe that's a should? Both parents should make expectations clear while understanding the other side might not follow them. In my opinion, people don't get to be mad about overstepped boundaries if the boundary was never made clear."*

Lauren T. (stepmom): *"Parents and stepparents should be respectful toward all involved caregivers of their child; whether it be an ex, a stepparent, an in-law, etc. Respect is important because everyone should be able to discuss matters with the other household* *(without starting a war) to provide consistency for the children. Even in a difference of opinion, even when you are hurting, it's important to act like an adult, take responsibility for your actions, and set a good example. Parents should always stop and think, 'Will this help my child? Does this directly affect my child?' If the answer is no, then they should reconsider their actions, words and decisions."*

Brynn (divorced mom, stepmom): *"Non-custodial parents should pay their child support on time. When he doesn't, I get grumpy."*

A.M. (divorced mom, stepmom): *"My stepchild's mom shouldn't feel entitled to know everything that goes on in our house, shouldn't feel entitled to comment on every little thing in a negative way or tell the kids what they can and cannot do at our house. It makes me feel like my house is not my own and it's very intrusive. Not being trusted is a terrible feeling too. Neither my husband nor I impose on our exes' homes like that."*

Katie S. (stepmom): *"If the pick-up spot is at school, then the other household should be informed if the child stays home sick, so they don't waste their time going to the school. In general, there should be a level of respect and common courtesy between households."*

J.L.D. (divorced mom): *"My child's stepmom should never directly insert herself and her opinions into the conversation that my child's father and I are having, regardless of what is being discussed."*

Linda T. (stepmom): *"Mom should not dictate who is allowed to attend the children's events. Mom should set a tone of courtesy and respect with the other household, so that her children know they are free to love everyone in both households, even if she can't* stand her ex or her child's stepmom. Mom should not use emotional blackmail to get her way with the kids regarding holiday schedules, birthdays, etc. Mom should follow the court order and put on a happy face for the kids when it's time to go to dad's house, even if she could get her way through emotional manipulation. Kids need their dads, too!"

Kelly (stepmom): "Parents should help prepare their kids for the world, instead of worrying about being their friend, because the child's lack of independence and responsibility affects their development. Parents should know and understand their custody order and be positive about it in front of the kids, because the kids seem to do better when they know what to expect and everyone is on the same page."

Jen (divorced mom): "My ex-husband should care more about our boys' education. He will fight me tooth and nail to have the right to make decisions (like which school they attend) but won't make sure their homework gets done on his night. He should prioritize essentials in the six hours he has them, instead of taking them swimming and letting them watch movies on a school night. Especially when he has them for the weekend two days later, he should save the "fun stuff" for then. Almost every week, he drops my boys off late, claiming to be doing homework. Then they will come home past bedtime with unfinished homework, not having taken a bath and sometimes without even eating a proper meal. I'm left scrambling to take care of the important stuff (food) and deciding what can slide (write a note to the teacher explaining what happened, instead of staying up all night to help them finish it and stressing out personally when it wasn't my fault). Having to let go of this sort of thing is the hardest part of parallel parenting for me."

K.K. (mom, stepmom): *"My baseline is that parents should put their own feelings aside to ensure that the children have a great relationship with each parent. If they don't like the new partner/wife/husband, they should keep that information to themselves and focus on encouraging the child to have a good time at the other house. Parents should also let the children know that not only will the parent be okay while the child is at the other house, the parent wants the child to have a wonderful time. My experience of having my stepchild's mom be unable to put her feelings aside to allow the children to have a relationship with their father is that the children suffer terribly. They act out at school and at mom's house. They lie. They tell their mom they want to stay with her, but then tell us they want to stay with us and sometimes refuse to get out of the car at her house. They make up lies about my children hurting them or being mean to them. It is hard for children to cope with their own conflicting loyalties, but when they have a parent who actively tries to turn them against the other house, it is destructive for the whole family."*

Harper (divorced mom, stepmom): *"I believe parents should never reprimand or otherwise cause a child to feel insecure or 'wrong' for loving the other parent or stepparent. That type of psychological warfare only destroys a child's sense of self and actually causes mistrust of the parent alienating the child. The only one truly hurt is the child, by the parent who claims to love them."*

Trish D. (divorced mom, stepmom): *"Parents should never tell a child to keep a secret from their other parent. This just sets the kid up to be vulnerable to predators."*

Rachel (stepmom): *"As a parent you should not put your ten-year-old, or any child, in the middle of adult conversations with the other parent."*

HOW "SHOULDS" SET YOU UP FOR DISAPPOINTMENT AND CONFLICT

So, do you find yourself wishing the other woman would behave differently? Wishing that she'd act more like *you* would in a particular situation? Do you want her to step up and conform to *your* idea of a good mother or stepmother? If you answered "yes" to any of these questions, then you're still *expecting* her to be someone she's not. You're putting the power for your happiness in her hands. Is that really where you want it to be? That's like being in a car with someone who drives like a maniac and hoping that if you give them enough instructions, they'll drive safely enough to keep both of you alive.

Her behaviors are patterns, just like yours. No amount of "wishing" is suddenly going to cause her to change, *just like she can't wish you into changing either.* The more you focus on getting her to behave in a way that you think is right, the weaker you actually are, because you are bent on controlling someone else's behavior when *they* are in charge of the outcome.

When someone has tried to control *you*, it hasn't gone well, has it? You may give in to please the other person, but resent it—or feel hurt and taken advantage of. Or you might harden yourself to hold your own. This can feel temporarily stronger, but ultimately, it creates distance and conflict between you and the other person, as you struggle not to feel anxious and unsafe.

It's hard enough to shape the behavior of our partners, our children, our stepchildren, and for some of us, even our pets. And those are the beings we love! Trying to modify the actions of someone we are already at odds with is like trying to build a castle out of runny sand. Behavioral changes just aren't going to hold together.

> **Kelli N. (divorced mom):** "*A five-year-old should be able to dress herself and pick out her own outfit, as she does when she is with me. At her dad's house, her stepmom picks out and changes my daughter's clothes. It makes me 'see' control issues that might not be there, but I pick up on it just because her stepmom does this.*"

Every time you have a firm "should" for the other household, you're setting an expectation. Any time you set an expectation and it's not met, you're going to be disappointed. Look at all the pressure we're under to meet our *own* expectations: *I should be thinner, I should be smarter, I should exercise more, I should be a more attentive mother or stepmother, I should have gotten that job, I should have spoken up, I should have my degree by now*—and on and on and on… all day, every day. What chance does *she* have?

Let's make some of the expectations running in the background of your life more visible, shall we?

QUIZ—ANY REASONABLE PERSON KNOWS THAT…

Circle the number that reflects how strongly you feel about this issue. (1 for not-so-much, 5 for off the charts)

A good mom is supposed to:	always put her kids first, no matter what 1 2 3 4 5	hold strong, even if the kids whine and complain 1 2 3 4 5
A good dad is supposed to:	be the consistent authority figure—and not their friend 1 2 3 4 5	always put his kids first, even above his marriage, if need be 1 2 3 4 5
A good stepmom is supposed to:	stay in the background for many years, until she's earned her involvement 1 2 3 4 5	be hands-on and involved since she's part of the family now 1 2 3 4 5
A good stepdad is supposed to:	just let mom handle everything since they're her kids 1 2 3 4 5	be an equal partner in parenting 1 2 3 4 5
Good kids are supposed to:	behave and always be respectful to the adults 1 2 3 4 5	be nurtured first if they're hurting and acting out 1 2 3 4 5

Good stepkids are supposed to:	give their stepmom a fair chance, especially if she's trying 1 2 3 4 5	only turn to their parents with important matters 1 2 3 4 5
A good husband is supposed to:	still provide for his children's mom, even if he is remarried 1 2 3 4 5	take care of his wife and his household only 1 2 3 4 5

How did you do? Are there certain statements that make you go "Damn right! And I'd be willing to arm wrestle you just to prove it!" Which ones and why?

_____

_____

_____

We appreciate the passion of your convictions! Only problem is when two people are both equally hopped up on adrenaline, it can make for a v-e-r-y long arm wrestling match. Something's gotta give. Now go back through each statement (you knew this was coming, right?) and try to imagine how *she* would rate each one. Insights?

_____

_____

_____

Where do all these "shoulds" stem from? One source is our values. Values are so ingrained and subconscious that we typically don't even realize what they are. We don't label them as such either. To us, our values are just common sense and the "right" way to do something.

VALUES: FUEL FOR THE FIRES OF CONFLICT

A value is *an internal judgment about what is important to an individual.* There are no morally right or wrong values. They're individual and a single value can mean different things to different people. Values are intangible; they are not something you do or have. *Meditation* is not a value, but it is an activity that may help one honor the value of *spirituality*.

For example, in divorce-connected families, one parent may often let the child stay home from school, driving the other parent nuts. One parent rates "education" and "responsibility" as two of their highest values, while the parent who frequently lets the child stay home from school values "freedom" and "independence." Can you see how this disparity sets up the two households for years of heated disagreements and confrontations?

IN THE WORDS OF OUR READERS

> **C.O. (stepmom):** *"Both parents should monitor schoolwork and cleanliness. It is really frustrating to have to deal with* all *the homework and get a prepubescent boy to understand daily hygiene. When he comes home, he's usually over-tired, it's almost bedtime, and he still has all the homework to get through. He then feels overwhelmed and resorts to pouting, crying, sighing, etc. We try to get through his homework without guiding him right to the answer to just get it done, while balancing which behavior corrections really matter at this point, and he's miserable. He doesn't retain anything from his homework. I find his behavior on those days annoying and I get frustrated. The cleanliness issue is annoying because we can't ever just pick him up and go do something. We have to factor in shower time because he might have gone three days without one or brushing his teeth. And this kid gets cavities. Our house pays for those bills and it feels like money wasted."*

> **Alissa B. (divorced mom):** *"A stepmom should keep her beliefs and views to herself in regards to religion, what's appropriate, kind of food to eat, etc., as it's mum and dad's job to mold our daughter into who we want her to be."*

> **Jean (stepmom):** *"Wholesome foods should be readily available for the children and mealtimes should be a time of daily connecting and sharing with each other. Sharing meals together is not a priority for the other household and food choices are more easy and casual there. We find we are having to compromise at the grocery store, because that is the diet the children are used to, since they are at*

*the other home more than here right now. We have to buy more
chips and junk food; things they know how to eat, or they will not
eat at all. Seriously."*

When another person violates one of your most important values, it can
feel extremely threatening, as if they are trying to tear down one of the most
important parts of your life. A large part of our behavior is based on an attempt
to honor and protect our values. When you're in a contentious situation, having an awareness of the hidden priorities at work will help you see the possible
rationale behind the other person's actions. We're not saying it's an excuse for
bad behavior, but often there's more to it than "She's such a bad parent!" or
"She's just trying to make life as difficult as possible for me!" or "She knows
exactly what she's doing!" Whether we realize it or not, we choose our priorities
in life by turning to the values we hold most dear.

Some examples of values are:

- independence
- inclusion
- acceptance
- intimacy
- predictability
- connection
- responsibility

JOURNAL QUESTIONS
WHAT'S IMPORTANT TO ME?

1. What are your top five most important values?

1. _____

2. _____

3. _____

4. _____

5. _____

2. Think about some common areas of conflict with the other household. In which areas is the cause of conflict actually a conflict of **values** between households?

_____

_____

_____

AS WE LEAVE THIS CHAPTER

After working through this chapter, can you see how your previously hidden assumptions are causing you to hold on to a reality that actually conflicts with, well, *reality*? Hopefully you now have greater insight into the latent expectations you act from and how they contribute to the strife between your two families.

In Section Three on this topic, we'll show you how to adjust your expectations so they're more in alignment with what is. You'll learn how to take control of what's actually within your power and let go of what's not.

CHAPTER 5

SELF-WORTH: WHY DOES THIS MAKE
ME FEEL SO LOUSY ABOUT MYSELF?
(letting her determine your self-esteem vs. generating your own)

THE TRICKY FEEDBACK LOOP OF SELF-ESTEEM

Ever had this happen to you? Your life is rich in friends and family who accept and appreciate you, but one day you hear a comment from someone who *doesn't*. Suddenly, you're obsessed, hurt and wondering "*Why? What's wrong with me? Do they see something that's secretly bad in me that everyone else can't?*" Forget all the people who *do* love you. A part of you will not rest until you change this *one person's* mind!

Why do we sometimes elevate one person's perceptions above all others like this? According to author Alison Armstrong, women are primarily externally motivated. When we think someone else doesn't approve of us, we feel driven to fix their opinion because we're basing our self-worth on their perceptions. Men, on the other hand, are traditionally internally motivated (even though they're also highly conscious of where they stand on the totem pole of status). They mostly measure themselves against *their* personal best.

There are two big problems for women with this tiring dance of pleasing others. First, you cannot give to others in a healthy way *without loving yourself first*. We're all sick of this cliché. But logically, how can you *love well* when you start from a base of feeling depleted and secretly needy—perhaps desperately so? (We've both been there, done that.)

Second, it's difficult to make changes in your life if you don't have a strong foundation of self-love. Think back to the last time you were sick in bed with a terrible cold or a serious injury. Were you at your best when you had major challenges to meet head on? Or did you long to retreat back under the covers until you returned to normal? Self-esteem gaps make conflict with other people extra difficult in the same way that having the flu makes getting up to pee seem like you're climbing Mount Everest. You're more susceptible to perceived insults and slights. You're more likely to obsess over events outside your control, be consumed by jealousy, or just feel hopelessly awful about yourself, like a pilot in a downward spin, unable to pull out.

Of course, from the outside, it doesn't *seem* like our sense of self-worth has anything to do with problems with the other house or the other woman. But look at the converse to test the hypothesis. When you're feeling great about yourself, don't life's challenges tend to bounce off of you with a satisfying "Ping!"?

We'll help you create more of that lovely sound here and with tools in Section Three.

IN JENNA'S WORDS

Anyone who has ever had an adverse relationship with the "other woman" knows the constant stress of another person having such a huge impact on your life is *exhausting*. Being part of a divorce-connected family is not for the faint of heart. If you don't have a strong sense of self, you're going to find this ride pretty damn challenging.

I'm thankful I had a good idea of who I was and wasn't by the time I met my husband. When I look back at myself in my early twenties, I cringe to think if I was still that girl, I could *never* have survived being a stepmom. Before, I was that typical girl looking to *others* to make me feel special. If someone didn't want me I was unhappy. But while dating, I was so jealous because, *oh my God*, if they ever left me, then what would that mean about me? I'd be back to feeling like I didn't matter, so I had to control everything. I remember being at the grocery store with my then-boyfriend and watching the checkout girl to make sure she wasn't eyeing him for too long.

That was a low point for me and mortifying now to think about, but feeling needy and out of control like that was a daily part of my life. I hated it. I even sought counseling, but when the therapist recommended Prozac at the end of my first session, I declined the offer and never returned. It wouldn't be until I found a wonderful therapist years later that I was able to address my more fundamental issues. My relationship with myself completely changed. I started trusting my decisions. I surrounded myself with people who supported my growth and independence and got rid of anyone who treated me poorly. *I treated myself* the way I wanted others to treat me: with love. I was kind to myself and said "no" to others when I knew saying "yes" would be detrimental to my well-being.

Then, I met my husband.

Boy, did this stepfamily business put all those wonderful therapy sessions to the test! That's why when I think back to whom I used to be, I know a small, jealous, insecure person could never survive the difficulties that we face in blended families. When it *feels* like you're being constantly scrutinized, it takes all the restraint in the world not to spend every minute of every day defending yourself. If your sense of self is shaky, you will require the approval of others to feel validated because it feels vital to your survival. Feeling strongly rooted in myself is one of the main reasons I've survived this challenge.

IN JENNIFER'S WORDS

When the first book (*No One's the Bitch*, co-written with Carol Marine, stepmom to my kids) came out with a big bang, life seemed full of promise. Around this time, I received a bizarre message from our publisher. They forwarded a short email from my first "real" boyfriend when I had lived overseas. He was the one I had fallen for in that hopeless, puppy-love way. Back then, I kept thinking *Really? You want me?* And then he pulverized my adolescent heart by breaking up with me at a very public event, after showing up hours late, stoned. I was baffled and devastated.

I cried over him for a long time. A few times a decade, I would dream about him, asking him why he had done what he'd done. He was a random phantom, bumbling around in my psyche. I never thought I'd see him again in real life, much less have him contact me. He represented one of the most hurtful rejections of my life and in low moments, he also represented my ultimate unworthiness. To hear from him after so many years later was surreal.

I wrote him a short, friendly, but formal message and when I received his direct reply, I had to laugh. His email was such a transparent effort to *start something up* that I scoffed at his clumsy attempt. He didn't even know me! It was like hitting on a perfect stranger.

And yet, another part of me was flattered, excited and *alarmed* because I knew through our alumni grapevine (go Facebook) that he'd been dating someone else long-distance, long-term. So why was he contacting me?

Let's just summarize a ridiculous episode in my life where I proceeded to lose all sense of judgment. Despite some red flags that were practically on fire like Tiki torches that could be seen from outer space, I believed his story about when things were over with his recent flame. At least, I *chose* to believe him in a way that I'm still embarrassed to admit because his story had enough holes in it to qualify as Swiss cheese. We started seeing each other long-distance and in person.

But as I soon discovered, he had a temper and an irrational jealousy that rated off the charts. A few emotionally exhausting months later, he abruptly dropped me when I demanded more clarification on when, exactly, his previous relationship had ended. He never spoke to me again and simply picked back up with his ex a few months later.

I was left alternately wondering how something so glorious and meant-to-be could have possibly ended, and why I was self-deluded enough to think it *was* even a relationship at all. His second rejection touched on something deep inside of me that was obviously *still* in need of healing. I consciously decided enough is enough! I would turn and face all those old, self-sabotaging patterns and take however long I needed *away* from relationships to understand what had happened—and why. Fast forward four years later. What I discovered after three years of being single is what led me to where I am today, in the happiest, easiest, most solid relationship I've ever had.

WHY WE RESIST LOOKING TOO DEEPLY AT SELF-LOVE

We're hoping this won't be the chapter you skip because it makes you squirm. Who likes discussing self-love? Sounds like we're either talking about masturbation or something cheesy you learned about in 7th grade health class.

Somehow, self-esteem is just inherently embarrassing. Pulling back the curtain on the way we feel about ourselves is a social taboo because the way we present ourselves publicly is *supposed to be* "the truth" about who we are. If we dig too deeply will we discover that we're actually conjuring up a version of ourselves that's closer to a lie? What do we do then?

We all want to be held in high esteem because, to our cavewoman brains, the issue is all tangled up with saber-toothed tigers, caves and a reliable water supply. Long ago, we needed others to help us stay alive, to find food and fend off predators. It was much more effective if we did this *together*. Doing everything alone would have likely equaled death. Aside from the simple issue of survival, we also tend to resist looking at any problems we might have with self-love and acceptance because:

- They seem too big and overwhelming to heal. Where do you start? What if nothing works?
- In a twisted kind of circular logic, the very fact that you're lacking self-esteem seems to *prove* your deepest fears about secretly being a loser.
- We already know our lack of self-love makes us needy in relationships, which is also embarrassing. Better to be in denial!
- We're afraid of "waking up" and realizing we're not living the life we want to be living. Find a new career? Leave your partner? Overhauling your life is disorienting and scary.
- Changing something in our lives means our dynamic with the people closest to us will change too. What kind of conflict might *that* cause?

A DEFINITION

Just to make sure we're all on the same page, let's define what we're talking about. Self-worth is a combination of many factors that result in an overall feeling of *authenticity and acceptance about who you are*. We know it when we see it, but here are the main ingredients. You have:

- the feeling you're living *your* life, not the life someone else wants you to live, such as parents, partner, friends, society, etc.
- a sense of competence and control over your life and destiny
- the ability to not take the behavior of others personally

- the feeling of deserving love from friends, family, a romantic partner
- trust in your ability to make good choices and decisions
- compassion and forgiveness for yourself when you're hurting or have failed in some way
- understanding for the mistakes of others and the role our egos play in how we relate to each other
- a good feeling about being open to others and risking your heart
- just the simple, solid feeling that you're really being you

In The Words Of Our Readers

Brittany (mom, stepmom): *"As women, we sometimes feel like we need to take care of everyone and put our needs last. I have done this many times and end up feeling resentful and irritable. When I take better care of myself, I'm able to take better care of everyone and be a happier mom!"*

Meg (stepmom): *"Am I the only one who thinks of pleasuring oneself when I hear "self-love!"*

Alanna (stepmom): *"I'll admit I find the term 'self-love' a bit cheesy, but it is essential for our relationships that we love and accept who we are right now. It's what allows us to truly love and accept others. In a blended family, there are so many people with different needs that it's easy to put our own needs on the back burner. But doing that only breeds resentment, anger, and isolation. We have to love ourselves enough to set aside time for self-care, so we can manage the stresses of this crazy, beautiful stepfamily dynamic."*

Kelli N. (divorced mom): *"After being in this group, I think of it as self-care, but before my experience here, if I had heard this, I'd of thought anyone 'loving' themselves would be selfish and conceited. As women we're taught from a young age to please others, be polite and to put ourselves last. Even if our moms weren't intending* *on sending us that message, we subconsciously picked up on it by watching her put everyone before herself. If my Mom was being good to herself, it was after I went to bed or before I woke up. Any of the in-between times I saw her take care of all of us kids, as well as my Dad. Now that I think about it, I bet my daughter sees me in that role as well, since my 'me' time is after she's gone to sleep for the night, or when she's at school."*

Anonymous (stepmom): *"Yep, what Meg said. Masturbation."*

K.K. (divorced mom, stepmom): *"I'm not that keen on the term 'self-love' since I think it has too many negative connotations. The concept is great, because if we are unable to love and accept ourselves, how can we reasonably expect that from someone else? I would use terms like self-acceptance, self-awareness and self-care."*

SURVEY: WHAT'S YOUR CURRENT BASELINE?

What do you think about your self-esteem at the moment? Let's evaluate where you are now and how that manifests itself with other people in your life. Which of these thoughts below are most familiar to you? Put a checkmark next to the ones that characterize how you typically handle your needs:

There will be time for me to relax later. It's more important for me to get everything done: attend Johnny's baseball game, take Katie to her swimming lessons, cook dinner, sort the laundry, get the kids ready for sleep, etc.

Versus

I have a million things to do, but I notice my stress levels are climbing into the stratosphere, so I'm going to take ten minutes to catch my breath, even if it kills me.

When I'm feeling overwhelmed or stressed, I often think 'How can I think of myself at a time like this? Money is tight and my partner is working as hard as he can. What right do I have to complain?'

Versus

We all have our challenges. My partner is overworked and needs some relief, but so do I. I'll ask him for some time to discuss how we can better meet each other's needs—and our own.

I can't remember the last time I did something fun for myself, outside of the family.

Versus

Ooh, it's girl's night! I love my weekly get-together with friends where I forget all about life's stressors!

I have to pee, but it can wait until my bladder feels like it's going to explode.

Versus

I need to pee! I'm going to take care of that right away so I'm comfortable and bladder infection-free.

How'd you do? Do you regularly honor your own needs or do you typically put them on the back burner? If you're a back-burner kind of gal, don't worry. In Section Three on Self-Worth we're going to show you how to start taking better care of yourself, without the guilt.

IN THE WORDS OF OUR READERS

A.W. (divorced mom, stepmom): *"When it comes to self-care, I can be pretty bad at remembering that I have needs too. I spend a lot of time on others' needs, to my own detriment. However, there are times when I stop to read my book or play my guitar and take time for me. I cherish those times, because while my kids are older and more self-sufficient, they are also more involved in sports, school activities and socialising and I am their taxi! I am very fortunate too, to have a husband who often sees my needs before I do and is happy to do a load or two of washing, or vacuum, just to ease the burden."*

Pat (stepmom): *"My 15-year-old stepson (whom I have known for 7 years) recently asked, 'Since when do you listen to country music?' to which I responded, 'Since I stopped caring about everyone's happiness more than my own.' That sums it up. I have spent a huge amount of time as a stepmom worrying about everyone else's happiness, even with the little things like what radio station is on in the car. Now, I hope I have a more balanced approach."*

CONSEQUENCES THAT FEEL JUST AWFUL: WHY SELF-LOVE MATTERS

Why does it matter how much we do or don't love ourselves? Doesn't everyone have *some* insecurity if you dig deep enough? Of course, they do. It's called *being human.* The problem is when you're not operating from a strong, solid base, you can end up like the Leaning Tower of Piza, precariously balanced and vulnerable to toppling over completely. We're susceptible to experiencing bouts of:

- **Overwhelming insecurity and low self-confidence:** It's common to experience these feelings periodically, but when they overshadow everything else, you're in need of healing. You might constantly compare yourself to others, thinking *What does she have that I don't?* Moms might be jealous because her ex seems to be a better husband to his current wife. Stepmoms might be jealous because it seems like mom got all the "firsts."
- **Craving validation:** Do you find yourself longing for acknowledgment for your hard work or sacrifices? If you don't have a core belief that you're worthy and lovable, you'll end up putting that responsibility on someone else's shoulders. That means *they're* the ones who have the power to make that happen. Not you.
- **Taking everything too personally:** How many times has the other woman complained about you or looked at you the wrong way? What about the events you actually took as insults, only to find out later that they weren't? People often don't spend as much time thinking about us as *we think* they do.

- **Changing who we are to suit others:** Perhaps you have a pattern of keeping requests to yourself or changing your opinion when speaking to people whose approval you crave. Their needs become more important, but in the process, you're selling yourself out. We all recognize behavior like this when a woman starts dating a man. Suddenly, she'll tolerate whatever music he likes and start eating foods she hates just because they happen to be his favorites. This can also continue into the marriage, and before the woman knows it, she's lost herself.
- **Continually doubting love from others:** If we don't feel worthy of love, we will sabotage relationships to prove our subconscious beliefs "right." We will have such a difficult time believing that our loved ones see the real us *and* still want us that we'll unknowingly work very hard to get our outward reality to match what feels "true" inside. For instance, our partner may be doing everything in his power to please us, but we'll still question his intentions. It's like that old Groucho Marx saying about not wanting to belong to any club that would have you as a member.

MOST OF OUR PAIN COMES FROM WHAT WE DO TO OURSELVES

When we hear the word "abandonment" we usually think of someone being left behind by another. A parent walking away from a young child. A husband leaving his vulnerable wife. But did you know that the person most likely to abandon you is *you*?

We look at the behavior of those around us and see it as the root cause of our pain. The truth is if we're feeling bad, it's likely we haven't been treating *ourselves* with loving-kindness. Habitually judging ourselves harshly can generate a free-floating shame that constantly hums along in the backgrounds of our daily lives. At its heart, shame is a feeling of intense unworthiness, of *being* bad to your very core. Any person believing that "fact" would feel powerless, hopeless and alone. Rejecting and abandoning ourselves this way feels simply awful.

Sadly, shame and *fear* go hand in hand. As we attempt to hide our low self-worth, we strengthen the underlying problem and turn ourselves into emotional pretzels: hiding our shame at feeling shame only leads to more shame! If we can back up and reassure ourselves with the thought that we're only one of millions of people experiencing a misdirected lack of self-love, we can peel back the layers of our corrosive feelings, see how they are self-perpetuating, and learn to break the cycle.

To summarize, we actively abandon ourselves by:

- making others' needs and feelings more important than our own
- ignoring our feelings of powerlessness, sadness, and hurt instead of acknowledging and tending to them, as we would with an upset child
- numbing ourselves through addictive behaviors, such as overeating, getting lost online for hours, watching too much TV, over-spending, alcohol or substance abuse, etc.
- believing our exaggerated, false beliefs about ourselves without question (for example: we're just *irredeemably* bad and unlovable)
- overscheduling our lives so we don't have time to practice good self-care or face painful emotions

It's your job—and no one else's—to address the varied and creative ways you treat yourself harshly and without kindness. As a matter of fact, it's actually not *possible* for someone else to heal you, even if they devote their entire life to doing so. How could that possibly work anyway? Another person tracking your every move—in the shower, by your bedside, while you eat breakfast or do your job, whispering affirmations you thought were completely bogus? Transformation comes *from within*. In Section Three we're going to show you how, even if it just starts with baby steps.

(For in-depth support on self-abandonment, we refer you to the Inner Bonding guru, Margaret Paul, PhD. She's the co-author of *Healing Your Aloneness*. You can find detailed information at **www.innerbonding.com.**)

THE BENEFITS OF ACTING FROM A FOUNDATION OF SELF-LOVE

When you practice self-love and start meeting more of your own needs, your entire life can change. Over time, you'll *expect* to be treated with respect because you're already treating yourself that way. Anything else will stand out as an aberration and becomes easier to recognize and step *around*.

One of the most beneficial skills you can learn is how to not take other people's behavior personally. For example, let's say the other woman accuses you of lying. If you know in your *heart* that you've done nothing to warrant such an accusation, you can stay calm and let her words roll off your back. "Huh," you say, "it's too bad she sees me that way. I wonder why…" Then you shrug your shoulders and go about your day unruffled, knowing that whatever she is struggling with is *her* problem. Your priority is maintaining alignment with your own values about how to treat people. There is no underlying anxiety, anger, or the feeling that you can't rest if she doesn't change her mind and see the *truth* about you. It's more likely that you'll respond to her with curiosity than aggression.

Most people think they have to wait until all their external problems are gone before they can start feeling better about themselves. Not true, because your life will never be 100 percent resolved. We know it's possible to set a new baseline of confidence for yourself because we've both done it (and continue to learn there's always work to be done on deeper levels). Don't wait until circumstances outside your control are neatly wrapped up before you allow yourself to feel good in your own skin. Don't put your life on hold until you get some vague, elusive approval from the world. You don't need anyone's permission to begin. Validate yourself!

When we're practicing self-love:

- **We take ownership of our own problems:** We separate someone else's pain from ours. We can determine what our responsibility is and what is theirs. We can detach with love. True, those lines get blurry when we see a loved one struggling and in pain, but it's easier to not take on the burdens that don't really belong to us when we feel grounded and "ourselves."
- **We can directly ask for what we need, instead of silencing ourselves:** Instead of fear and trying to control the situation by manipulating others, our actions can come from love—for ourselves and others. We're not running from the possibility of rejection. We have the strength to ask for what we want without

attachment to the outcome, using passive-aggressive behavior or hoping someone will rescue us from being a victim. If it doesn't work, you don't get indignant. You simply accept it and think of a Plan B. You're more likely to address negative behavior in a non-threatening manner, which helps others to respond without feeling defensive.

- **We are able to self-soothe:** We're able to make ourselves feel better instead of looking to outside sources. We take it upon ourselves to calm our emotions down and regain our stability. We see situations with more objectivity. When we know that we have already done the work of tending to our upset feelings, we come to the other person with our cup mostly full, instead of mostly empty.

- **We can forgive our own mistakes:** Forgiveness makes room for change and forward progress. When you increase the well of compassion you have for yourself, it makes you a more mature, adaptable person. You surrender to the vagaries of life that can't be reduced to black-and-white problems, with one person in the wrong and one who's obviously right. To the extent that you can accept and even embrace your own contradictions and foibles, it's easier to accept the same in others and empathize with their ongoing struggles, even if it involves being on the receiving end of negative behavior. Forgiving ourselves is often last on our list of tasks when we're in conflict, but it's one of the most powerful ways to transform a difficult situation.

REACHING OUT TO THE OTHER WOMAN—OR NOT

When you have a foundation of steady self-assurance, you can act upon the occasional impulse to forge a better relationship with the other woman, without being attached to a positive result. But if your worth as a person hangs on whether or not she responds positively to you, you'll never reach out (even if the time is right—or if you do, you'll drive yourself crazy waiting for her response). When you don't *need* her approval, you can extend an olive branch with an open heart, free from manipulation.

SKIRTS AT WAR | 79

Thinking it will be a cold day in hell before you reach out? That's okay too. You'll make that decision not because you're angry, resentful or feeling spiteful, but because you're treating yourself with love and respect. You may decide that working on an active partnership with your counterpart isn't a stress you want in your life.

AS WE LEAVE THIS CHAPTER

While it may be uncomfortable to be honest about the ways you haven't been very kind or caring toward yourself, once you do, so many other things in your life will start to fall into place, including the way you relate to people and the nourishment you allow yourself to soak up from your relationships.

You'll also find your expectation of how others treat you improves. Behaviors you once "put up with" become unacceptable as you start to realize your inherent worth.

In the next chapter on boundaries, we'll focus on the ins and outs of unwanted behavior from the not-so-well-behaved people in your life.

CHAPTER 6

BOUNDARIES: HOW DO I KEEP HER OUT OF MY BUSINESS?

(overdoing and unprotected vs. clear, consistent boundaries)

TEACHING OTHERS HOW TO TREAT YOU

Wouldn't it be great if there were a secret weapon for keeping the other woman (and the other household) from having a direct impact on your day-to-day well-being? While there's no ray gun that will instantly transform someone from high-conflict to Zen master, there is something you can use that's pretty darned effective.

The word "boundaries" gets thrown around a lot these days like a self-help gimmick destined to blast through the other person's crappy behavior and shield you from all future harm, guaranteed! The truth is it's one of the most misunderstood concepts in interpersonal relationships and most people don't know how to use them to their full potential. They're not magically effective techniques that can seduce someone into behaving cooperatively. They're not cleverly phrased threats that can coerce people into acting against their will. And they don't get automatic results, no matter how correctly you apply them.

However, when used conscientiously, boundaries can provide you with distance and protection from unwanted behavior, but you must continue to customize them for your unique situation until you find what works. Boundaries are essential because as long as you don't clearly and consistently say, "Stop it!" others will continue to treat you in the same, unwanted manner.

In this chapter, you'll learn how to diagnose the *efficiency* of the limits you're imposing on other people. Where are you sending unclear messages or unintentionally inviting the other party to misbehave? Doing too much for others, unprompted, is also related to poorly placed boundaries. (In Chapter 13's *Making Progress* section for boundaries, we'll show you how to set them and how to enforce them.)

Here are a few of the benefits strong boundaries can create in your life:

- They can protect every potential area of your life: money, time, energy, relationships, the consistency of your day, etc. Nothing is exempt.
- They allow positive elements in, while keeping harmful elements out, helping you feel safe in your environment.
- They help you exhibit *self-respect*, regardless of the level of disrespect shown to you by others.
- They help you clarify your needs, so they can actually be met.
- They encourage you to balance your responsibilities and place the burden for them where they should be: on your shoulders, not someone else's.
- By the same token, they help you place the responsibilities of others squarely on their shoulders.

Think of them in two ways. Clear, crisp boundaries are great for addressing situations in which you're either *under-protected* (like a turtle without a shell) or *overdoing* (like a long-suffering, very tired turtle completing a marathon). But if you want to use this peace-generating technique correctly, you're going to have to fluff up your confidence and overcome some ingrained fears about possibly pissing some people off.

Think you're up for it? Then read on.

IN JENNA'S WORDS

Years ago, I was working for a wonderful doctor as a chemotherapy nurse. It was a small office he shared with his wife, who was also a doctor. Things went well for about a year. Then my boss's wife started accusing me of things I wasn't doing, such as ignoring her patients when I passed them in the hall (absurd) and being rude to her patients (even more absurd). She became impossible to be around. Her accusations continued and she became verbally aggressive with me.

For whatever reason, she had formed particular beliefs about who I was and then acted on them. Although I could see no evidence for her beliefs, her mentality must have served her in some way because there was nothing I could do to change her mind. She knew the "truth" about me and was sticking to it! This was the first time in my adult life that I'd ever encountered someone treating me like this, but it wouldn't be the last.

The experience was difficult because I loved my job, loved my patients, and felt lucky to have such a great boss. But when it came down to it, I knew I didn't deserve to be treated that way. I finally told my boss I was leaving and he begged me to stay. I distinctly remember him saying to me, "Can't you just ignore her?" I thought, *But what she's doing is so not okay! She's harassing me and I can't just ignore it. Nor should I have to.* I responded with, "Maybe *you* think it's acceptable to be treated that way because you've gotten used to it, but I'm not." A month later, I was gone. I heard through the grapevine a few years later he eventually divorced her.

In this situation, I refused to be treated like a doormat. I would not be the target of someone else's inner conflict. I put my well-being first and was able to extricate that person from my life. But in the mom/stepmom relationship, we're not lucky enough to have that option. So what's the answer? How do we keep someone out of our life when we're literally *stuck* with them? I decided I had to learn how to keep my husband's ex from affecting my life, *while in it.* It took a lot of trial and error, but I finally figured out that the best way to do that was by creating clearer boundaries, especially around communication. This goes to back to what we talked about in Chapter 5. Doing so is one of the ways I treat myself lovingly.

IN JENNIFER'S WORDS

Ironically, one of the consequences of getting along *better* with my ex and his wife, Carol, was that I needed to rethink how I approached boundaries between our two families. Once the adults became closer friends, it was great to be able to share family dinners, jokes, pow-wow about issues regarding the kids, and just generally confide in each other. After David and Carol's house burned to the ground in the Bastrop Complex fire of 2011, we even made a group decision to move to Oregon so our youngest daughter could still be near both sets of parents.

Close friends though we are, we've had our share of missteps and crossed wires between families. Occasionally, one of us will accidentally repeat something that has been said to us in confidence. All of us have made this mistake. Somehow, in the thick of developing storylines about problems and heightened emotions, we'd "forget" that what we now took as just part of the situation was a sentiment that our confidant didn't necessarily want everyone else to know. Then there would be backtracking, pained explanations, and having something out in the open that people weren't necessarily ready to discuss. Talk about complicated!

I can't speak for anyone else, but in retrospect, I think we've all (kids included) had to go through the process of taking a step back, adjusting our interactions, and creating a little buffer of protection. While the word "buffer" also implies "distance," I don't think it's been a bad thing by any means. Now that our daughters are both adults, we've had to realize that they have the right to expect privacy and to brainstorm or receive support for their concerns without everyone being aware of the various stages of their thought processes and emotions. It's been a clumsy road at times, but one that we needed to take as our children have grown up and their need for independence and discretion has changed.

THE SIMPLEST DEFINITION POSSIBLE

Some people use the word "boundary" as if they're proudly taking a stand for themselves and *sticking it* to the other person, but that's an inaccurate understanding of its function. A boundary is simply a limit you set with someone without any kind of assured response or reaction. It's a way of communicating to someone who is crossing a line. "If you continue this unwanted behavior, then *this* is how I will respond."

Since we can't control others (not even trained poodles or two year-olds!), we can only tell someone else what *we* will do. Read that part again! We're conveying to the other person how *we* will behave, *in advance*, if they continue to act in a destructive or harmful manner. They may not agree with us or our characterization of their behavior. They may not agree to our stated consequences either. Doesn't matter. What matters is the *consistency of our responses*.

Boundaries are this little back-and-forth dance, almost like a call-and-response section of a song. You communicate a boundary. The other person responds with a particular behavior, likely similar to the unwanted behavior they originally had. You impose your boundary. They react. You adhere to your boundary. They respond again. If their response is negative, repeat!

IN THE WORDS OF OUR READERS

> **Heather G. (divorced mom, stepmom):** *"One boundary I learned to set was that I was not going to communicate with my husband's ex-wife. For quite a while, that meant not going to exchanges because she couldn't handle me there and it caused too much drama. Did I have the right to go? Absolutely. Was it worth it for me to go and have the potential of setting her off (by me just being in the car), causing stress for my stepson? Nope. You have to pick your battles and it wasn't letting her 'win' or have her way, it was me taking care of myself and my family. I found other things to do with that time and enjoyed not having to worry about the drama."*

> **Peggy N. (divorced mom, stepmom):** *"I stopped saying 'yes' when I really meant 'No.' The rest of my boundaries are self-care related. My 'me' time is a no-trespass zone. A huge boundary my husband and I established in our home was our reconnect time and space after work. Junior was not allowed to infiltrate our couple bubble. Period. Best boundary ever."*

TYPES OF BOUNDARIES

Boundaries are not one-size-fits-all and they don't always look the same from the outside. They take on different qualities, customized to your ultimate goal. You will need to switch between the two boundaries listed below, depending upon the ages of the children, the state of cooperation between the two households, and the accumulation of other stresses in your life at the time.

AGREED-UPON BOUNDARIES

Some boundaries may require back-and-forth and compromise, but eventually you both come to an agreement after requesting changes in their behavior. We call this an "agreed-upon boundary." This is the most favorable type of boundary because it has the highest chance of being respected, since both parties are on the same page. An example of this might be asking the other household to call to speak to the kids at a set time in order to prevent disrupting your evening plans—and having the other household sign off, after discussing a few possibilities. Who would have thought life could be so easy!

PARALLEL BOUNDARIES

Then there is a boundary that one party sets, regardless of whether the other party is amenable. We call these "parallel boundaries." They're necessary when the other party is aggressive, unable to keep agreements, or perceived by you as a danger. They are the type most likely to anger the other person, but nevertheless must be implemented. An example of this would be you not responding to the other woman's emails or texts because they are consistently aggressive or insulting. She may continue to attempt to contact you, but you do not respond.

Parallel boundaries don't just come in handy when you're dealing with your enemies. Sometimes we need to set them with our loved ones too. For example, perhaps in order to save your peace of mind, you can no longer be the person responsible for doing your stepchild's homework with him. He's disrespectful, doesn't want to listen to you, and you're not welcome at the parent-teacher conferences. You've had it. Your husband isn't happy with your decision because he works long hours and is too tired when he gets home to address the homework issue. But you know if you give in, you'll end up resenting both him and your stepchild.

It may seem as if there's "no other choice" but for you to continue helping with the homework, right? But you know this is a decision you need to make for long-term peace in your family, regardless of whether your husband agrees in the short term. To help lessen the blow, you can offer to help your partner come up with other possibilities, such as an after-school tutor or perhaps an extra study class at school.

As interconnected family members, we often feel anxious about "not doing our part" and are eager to provide a solution before setting a limit that's vital to our sanity. *But making sure that another solution is available is not necessarily a prerequisite to instituting your boundary.* It's up to everyone involved to find an answer that works, not just you.

JOURNAL QUESTIONS:
HOW ARE MY BOUNDARIES WORKING?

Where are some areas where you're starting to suspect you have "leaky" boundaries, or perhaps even none at all?

_____
_____
_____

What are some boundaries that have actually worked well for you? (Good job!)

_____
_____
_____

WHAT DO BAD BOUNDARIES LOOK LIKE?

Once you start experimenting with healthy boundaries, you'll be able to spot rickety, ineffective ones a mile away. The tip-offs are that bad boundaries are:

- inconsistent
- unenforceable
- often created from a negative state of mind

INCONSISTENT

These are boundaries that you are wishy-washy about enforcing. They're limitations that are not communicated clearly. Sometimes you let the other person violate them and sometimes you don't. Ever tried to train a dog this way? What happens? A confused dog and an unhappy you.

Unenforceable

Bad boundaries are also presented in the form of trying to control another person by telling them what to do, instead of telling them what you will do: "Stop showing up at my house." "Stop emailing me." "Don't feed the kids hot dogs with MSG in them ever again!" These are *demands*, not boundaries. They usually don't go over well and *you can't ensure they will happen*, which is why they don't work.

What do we mean about them not being enforceable? Well, take the example of asking your counterpart not to show up at your house. Can you really and truly keep her from ever coming over again? Even if you erected a brick wall around the perimeter of your property, can you keep her away? Can you ensure that her car will die if it comes within twenty feet of your yard? Would a small army of trained Jack Russell terriers immediately yap her into submission? Not likely.

But you *can* tell her *what you will do* if she continues with her unwanted visits. "I will not answer the door if you come over. I will not interact with you in any way, shape, or form. If you continue to visit my house, I will call the police and remain inside until they arrive."

That's the difference.

Fear-Based Scenarios

Another form of bad boundaries is unenforceable boundaries created out of fear (kind of like consequences and punishments you create with misbehaving children that are impossible to implement): "Do not joke around with your stepmom when you're at your father's house." "I don't want you to even *think* about mentioning your mom's name while you're here!" Even if you found a way to enforce boundaries formed out of fear, they're not healthy. They alienate the positive people in your life, not just the harmful ones. They keep you stuck and focused on an obsessive cycle of helpless, endless negativity, instead of steering you in the direction of learning and growth.

When following through with boundaries, you need to think about them the same way you would if you were disciplining an unruly child, training an animal, or programming a computer. They must be clear and simple.

What Instructions Are You Creating For The Other Person—Both Spoken And Unspoken?

If you let someone violate an important boundary, even once, without conse-quence, you're teaching that person it's okay. You have basically communicated to them, without consciously intending to:

Fine. That is, in actuality, *how it's done. Please, push that much harder next time to get what you want, even though I told you not to. Just ignore what I said and act in accordance with how I actually* behave, *because that's the* real deal. *Don't mind me!*

So what are you *really* asking the people around you to do, if your behavior and corresponding reactions are part of the "instructions?" Okay, your turn now.

EXERCISE—BAD BEHAVIOR INSTRUCTIONS!

If you were going to write out bad boundary "instructions" for a difficult person in your life to behave *just as they currently are*, what would those instructions look like? In what way are you inadvertently communicating the wrong instructions? How are you, despite your best efforts, reinforcing her unwanted behavior with *your* responses? Let's look at an example:

> **Bad instructions:** *"Dear other woman, I want you to leave me alone and stay out of my family life. But please, keep emailing me every time you have a complaint about me. Don't forget to point out all my flaws and things you still hate about me from long ago. If I don't respond (but I might, sometimes!), just keep trying. I hope you'll remove yourself from my life because you're making me so miserable I can't stand it, but in the meantime, feel free to flood my inbox, because I'm reading every message. Ten times. No, make that twenty. Thanks!"*

> **Accidental reinforcements:** *"Even though I've asked her to leave me alone, I sometimes respond to her, when I've already told her I*

won't. So I'm not really keeping my word because I'm proving that I will still engage with her and keep this cycle going. Even though I've set up an email filter to send her messages to a delete folder, I still check it to see if she's sent me anything outrageous because I'm dying of curiosity to see what she wrote. I want to prove to myself that she's wrong and what she wrote is unacceptable. But then I read her messages and get upset, then feel like I can't just let her get away with talking to me that way. The drama just starts all over again as I reach my breaking point and ask her to leave me alone."

You try it. Have some fun! My bad instructions are:

_____
_____
_____

My accidental reinforcements are:

_____
_____
_____

Now, keep in mind, no one is perfect. There will be times when you will not enforce your boundaries consistently, especially in the beginning when you're learning how to put them into practice. We don't want you to beat yourself up for it later. You'll just need to recognize your mistakes, try to pinpoint what prevented you from enforcing the boundary, and brainstorm what you need to do differently next time. We'll get into the particulars in Section Three.

WHAT PREVENTS US FROM CREATING HEALTHY BOUNDARIES?

If boundaries are so great and awesome, why do we have so much trouble creating strong, clear limits with other people? Because we're afraid of the consequences! Women, in general, feel a strong need to be liked by everyone, whether we like the other person or not.

Another problem is the resistance we encounter from other people. What happens when someone tries to tell *us* what we can and can't do? Many of us get defensive, inwardly thinking, *You ain't the boss of me!* We push back against anyone trying to exert dominance over us, maneuvering to gain the upper hand—even if we do so later or by being passive-aggressive (an easier way to avoid direct confrontation). Teenagers know this mindset well, but so does anyone in a contentious relationship.

Fear is a major reason why women have so much trouble setting boundaries, and it comes in all sorts of lovely manifestations:

- Fear of saying "no"
- Fear of looking like a "bitch" or being too demanding
- Fear of hurting someone else's feelings
- Fear of starting conflict or perpetuating it
- Fear of making things worse
- Fear of creating more stress or hard work for someone else
- Fear of not being "worth" the extra trouble
- Fear that our loved ones won't love us anymore

Do any of these resonate with you? The next time you're faced with an uncomfortable situation and attempt to create a change, see if any of the fears above are surfacing and acknowledge yourself for your bravery. It takes *courage* to set a boundary because even though you may be afraid of these phantom consequences, you're taking a risk and moving forward anyway.

There's one more insidious motivation for not setting boundaries and it comes from a surprising source. It's got a fancy name that we made up, but we're sure you'll recognize it right away by its shorter description.

THE FEMININE MARTYR COMPLEX: OVERDOING

As women, we're constantly trying to anticipate what people need *and doing it before being asked* either as a show of love or perhaps because we feel pressured to fill a societal role. As a result, we're exhausted and we—and the people around us—suffer because of it. Overdoing for others is a strong symptom of a lack of boundaries.

Overdoing leads to feeling taken advantage of and breeds resentment, annoyance, and feeling overwhelmed. Are you performing "kindnesses" out of obligation? Are your actions fear based or are they done from generosity? Are you making an unspoken "trade" of sorts? *Let me do for you, so you will like me or love me.*

If you're making breakfast for everyone without anyone else who's old enough to do it ever reciprocating, if you're regularly shuttling kids off to school and it makes you late to work when they're fully capable of walking themselves, if you're making dinner and you're the only one who ever cleans up the dishes or pots and pans, if you're constantly picking up socks and underwear and wet towels from the floor, there's a very good chance you are overdoing.

So many actions that start from love can somehow end up becoming *expectations* on the part of others. Then, before we know it, we've created a sense of *entitlement* on the part of our children, stepchildren, and our partners.

We fear creating the space to let others do their duty as self-respecting, responsible family members (even a five-year-old can put their dirty dishes in the dishwasher or fold towels from the dryer, although maybe not very well!) because we don't want to seem selfish, petty, uncaring or, god forbid, unfeminine.

We yearn to take a moment for ourselves or delegate responsibilities, but pay a steep price for it in resentment and guilt. The hamster wheel starts up in our heads as we complain to ourselves that other people should be helping more, or doing what they're supposed to for their allowance, or how you have too much already on your shoulders. Then you move from that to thinking about how you want your children or stepchildren and your partner to feel like their house is a home, full of nurturing and warmth and "the little kindnesses." So you decide "Well, just this once, since they're having a rough week or a bad day…"

And on it continues.

HOW OVERDOING "FROM LOVE" CAN BACKFIRE

You may justify your actions by saying, "Hey, I'm tough. I can take it. I'm knowingly working this hard and I accept it." But consider what you might actually be *taking away* from other people in the process. Even though we have the best of intentions, here are some ways in which overdoing makes us (and others) crash and burn:

- The men in our lives long to feel useful, like their contributions mean something to us. But if we're doing everything for ourselves *and* everyone else, our man thinks he's not needed. This can be extremely emasculating. He may react by shutting down or ceasing to offer his help in the future. Don't take his ability to provide away from him!
- The other woman may be offended by all your overdoing. In fact, she might be insulted because she thinks you're trying to make her look bad. Sure, those are her insecurities at play, but by doing less you both win.
- There's a price you and your family pay for doing everything. Your energy is zapped. You're cranky. Everyone "expects" things of you now because that's what you've taught them to expect. You have no time for *you*. Perhaps your family has noticed you've been on edge lately and are losing your cool at the drop of the hat. They're walking on eggshells around you. Can you see how *no one* in the family benefits from your overdoing?
- You're taking away people's opportunities for growth and increased responsibility. Everyone needs to feel capable and competent. It's often through challenges and discomfort that we grow the most, feeling our way into new skills through failure, trial and error. Just because your husband, stepchild, young child, or teen is lousy at something and you can do it "right" doesn't mean you *should*. When will they get any better if you're always stepping up and doing it for them?

JOURNAL QUESTIONS:
WHERE AM I OVERDOING?

Food for thought, huh? Do you see how you might be reducing opportunities for growth and responsibility in your family? In what ways?

_____

_____

_____

AS WE LEAVE THIS CHAPTER

It wouldn't be very nice of us to give you permission to take a step back and create new habits in your household without showing you how, so in Section Three on boundaries we'll walk you through the specific steps for setting healthy limits. We'll also show you how to stop overdoing so you can feel more supported facing the everyday stressors in your divorce-connected family.

When you're able to say "no" to things you really don't want to do or to things that others should be doing for themselves, you end up feeling more empowered, even if nothing else in your life changes. You'll have more time for the things that feed your spirit and fill your emotional well, and you'll have more energy to nurture your relationships and those around you.

Now let's take a serious look at the tools and techniques that are going to serve you well on your journey to increased personal peace and more love in your family...

SECTION TWO
POWER TOOLS

CHAPTER 7

POWER TOOLS: HOW CAN I FEEL BETTER RIGHT NOW?

(unconscious habits vs. positive, deliberate action)

One of the hardest things about ongoing conflict with the other woman is the *net* effect that negative emotions have upon your psyche and your body. In this section, we'll provide you with tools to discharge those feelings, get out of a stress response, and back into a relaxation response to restore your natural equanimity. You'll find exercises to release resentment, anger, and powerlessness. We'll help you identify subconscious beliefs and "invisible drivers" that contribute to emotional distress so you can make more peaceful, *conscious* choices.

Unprocessed, difficult events can become cumulative. As old conflicts pile up, new upsetting experiences seem more intense than they probably should. In essence, you've become hyper-*sensitized* to future trauma, like a former soldier with Post-Traumatic Stress Disorder who jumps at every loud noise in a harmless environment.

We're used to referring to this cacophony of negativity as *stress,* but that term glosses over the painful reality of our day-to-day experiences. There's the deep hurt of being mistreated and the sharp-edged fear of more betrayals coming your way with no end in sight, making your spirit *ache.* It's having your weeks tinged with the aura of anxiety, it's the sick feeling of jealousy or being blatantly excluded, ruining moments that should be simple and happy. It's the boiling fury and resentment against wrongdoing that makes you feel weaker and smaller.

You *can* create a reliable effective strategy for releasing your troublesome emotions in the moment—or shortly thereafter. You can dismantle your "pile" of gunk by untangling the old knots and prevent new ones from forming. There are tricks and tools you can use on the fly or when you have quiet moments to go deeper. Either way, help is at hand.

IN JENNA'S WORDS

When I was younger, I was such a brat. Something would set me off and I'd scream and cry until I got my way. Once, when I was thirteen, my mom made plans for me to babysit (which I hated). I went from sweet to raging child in a flash like a switch had flicked inside of me. That "out of control" feeling was the worst. I would feel so powerless, like *I needed the other person to stop* in order for me to feel better. But I couldn't control them. No amount of crying or screaming could, either.

As an adult with the ability to evaluate my behaviors and the emotions behind them, I realized I would get triggered when I perceived something as unfair. I *had* to make it right. I *had* to be in control of the situation. Well, I couldn't go through life like that—having a tantrum every time I thought something was unjust or I felt threatened—so I sought to figure out how to better control my reactions.

They don't call it personal "growth" for the hell of it. After immersing myself in self-improvement books, I learned how to feel like a whole person all on my own. I no longer needed external circumstances to be "perfect" to feel at peace. At the same time, since I was only depending on myself for my happiness, when something set me off, I didn't have to raise my voice, be rude or insult the offender. I stopped taking everything so personally. When someone acted out toward me, I viewed them with compassion instead of anger.

It felt pretty amazing to get to that point, but then I became a stepmom and I experienced periods of regression. Five years later, I now realize this is just the nature of the beast. I can be feeling great for months, coping with all sorts of stressors and then BAM!, something totally throws me off. From my experience, I suggest you expect to get diverted periodically on your path to peace. But don't get discouraged, the diversion is only temporary. Hopefully some of the healing techniques in this section will resonate with you and enable you to course correct during those times.

IN JENNIFER'S WORDS

In January of 2011, I finally did the one thing I didn't want to do for fear of the humiliation. I declared bankruptcy. Doing so seemed like the final nail in the coffin of my recent failures. I felt like a total fuck-up. I had failed with the book since I hadn't made any money off of it besides the original advance from 2008. I'd worked on it for years, then accrued massive credit card debt while I focused on marketing it and making it a success. I had failed as a writer and with relationships—as a grown-up who was supposed to be in control of my life.

Of course, there were other areas of my life where I *wasn't* failing. Motherhood. Close friendships. Exercising daily and eating right. Those are important parts of my life too, but like most humans, I took my accomplishments there for granted. With money and romance, I felt like a total loser. Not only that, I felt as if I had to hide the truth of my situation, lest I undo any of the status I had built up as a writer, as an "expert" of anything. But here's the thing. You cannot really be who you are if you are lying to yourself and the world, if you are propping up a facsimile of yourself, a facade. You have to keep track of two versions of yourself. You can't move forward with pure, straight-out momentum. You are torn, in limbo between current pain and future promise, between regret and change, between fear and hope.

In pointing to all the reasons for why things had gone so poorly, I believed a bunch of lies that fueled bitterness and self-pity. (Always such an attractive quality, huh?) *The book should have done well since I wrote it from the heart and it was meant to help people. I tried so hard, I risked so much. If I took that big of a leap of faith, it should have panned out just like in the movies.*

I also believed some big lies about what was wrong with me. What was wrong with others. And lies about how everything *should* have gone. *I mess up everything big. Something is very wrong with me. I can't trust the world or other people. I can't trust life. Things are always going to end in failure. No one will ever truly love me.*

If you're appalled, thinking that such extreme, pathetic statements couldn't possibly apply to you, or conversely, apply all too well, let me just say that the whole point of this story is that having these two areas of my life come crashing down around me was a great opportunity to get to the heart of what I was telling myself.

Because of the primary beliefs I had about who I am and how the world works, I made decisions that created pain, shame, chaos and some cringe-worthy stories that, thank God, I can now laugh at and learn from. Sorting through those beliefs, taking ownership of them, and working diligently and honestly to transform them was the only way to move forward—unless I wanted more of the same.

It was only when I could see those blatant misrepresentations of reality for what they were that some of my other "surface" attempts to feel any better *really* started working. In this chapter, we'll talk about how to get the most out of both kinds of resources.

And now, back to you!

UNDER ASSAULT

You're going to see the other woman at an after-school activity or maybe it's the first time you're doing a drop-off or pick-up alone, just the two of you. Your history with her has been rocky. You feel like everything you do, no matter how innocuous, ends up being evaluated by the other household and found lacking—especially things that seemed just fine before by your standards and those around you.

Stepmoms, maybe she's sent you nasty texts or email messages, or repeatedly calls you the "other woman," even though you met years after their split. Moms, perhaps she likes to "show" the kids how much better she is than you at a variety of things or has let people believe *she's* the mom by not correcting anyone who refers to her as such in public. Whatever your personal story entails, you've been there—sweaty palms, heart racing, knees nearly shaking uncontrollably, visions in your mind of a cat-fight in front of strangers. All this at the thought of the unknown, the thought of being face-to-face with this larger-than-life creature who has made your life so difficult.

Have you ever felt threatened or attacked by the other woman and reacted by yelling or sending an email that was equally as pissy as hers? In the moment you may have felt justified. After all, it feels good to protect yourself, right? But then, after you calmed down, did you regret your response? Feel embarrassed? Become angry with yourself for letting her get to you? For acting like *her*? Such

...controllable, about-to-lose-it ...some situation is just physiology at work. Phew. And here you thought you were losing your mind, when really, you just got bumped into stress-response mode because of a very real process going on in your brain and body. Let's talk about the physical and emotional effects the stress response can have on you:

PHYSICAL EFFECTS

When we perceive danger, our bodies produce the fight, flight or freeze response in order to help us respond to the threat. Hormones (adrenaline and cortisol) are released by our adrenal glands, which cause increased heart rate, muscle tension, and acute concentration. After the threat is gone, our bodies are supposed to *relax* and return to a normal resting state (the relaxation response). Our bodies are designed to be self-healing *while in the relaxation response*. Remember that part.

The problem is, faced with everyday stressors, many of us remain on "high alert," which is definitely not good for our bodies. It's worth noting that when you relive an upsetting event in your mind, *your body doesn't know* it's just a memory. It doesn't know the difference! Physically, you are reacting as if the negative memory is happening in this moment, continuing and prolonging the effects of stress on your body.

Think back on the last time you were ill. In this weakened state, you may have noticed that if you slid into a spiral of negative thinking, you actually felt much worse physically. If you received some unexpected happy news or even a simple act of kindness, suddenly you felt much better. It goes both ways. Our bodies are highly tuned to the radio station of our emotions, like it or not.

You're also sending the two parts of your nervous system (the sympathetic and parasympathetic) two very conflicting messages. The sympathetic part of your nervous system is like the accelerator in a car, trying to rev you up and make you "go" (and attack the problem) when trouble strikes. The parasympathetic part serves as the brakes, trying to get you to calm down, relax and decompress. When you're highly stressed both parts of your nervous system, the accelerator and the brakes, are struggling for dominance. Remember what it's like to be desperate for sleep, but have your mind racing as you mentally replay the latest conflict with the other house? That's it in a nutshell. Feels awful.

A JAMMED AMYGDALA

Your amygdala is one of the oldest, most primitive parts of your brain. Its job is to detect and process fear and threats to help you stay alive. It's the part of your brain that sees a wavy line in the grass and instantly makes you jump before your conscious brain even has time to *consider* the word "Snake!" Your amygdala keeps you on high alert so you'll stay away from danger and anything that might end your life prematurely.

Usually, we can coast along, trusting our ever-ready amygdala to do its thing in the background, like having a totally hot medieval guard outside the castle door of your chamber who never sleeps. But problems arise when you feel as if you're under *continual assault* by the other woman or the other household. Suddenly, your amygdala becomes not such a good friend. Instead of keeping the threats in your life in perspective, now it seems like things are always bad, always reason to be on your toes. You feel unable to catch your breath and *regroup* and you're not spending much time in the pre-frontal cortex part of your brain, where problem solving takes place. Instead of the super-buff medieval guard, your amygdala has now become the oppressive, totally un-hot prison warden, breathing too loudly at your door, jangling his keys.

When your amygdala is being "hijacked" you feel unable to think clearly, as if you have tunnel vision. You'll have trouble seeing the bigger picture or other perspectives. Your brainstorming abilities go out the window. You become defensive and *need* to prove you're right, which keeps you feeling stuck and powerless. As we mentioned before, one of the biggest problems with our emotions is that the intensity of our feelings *makes our beliefs* feel *as if they're true*—when they might not be at all! Think back to a time when you were absolutely certain you were right, and then the facts proved otherwise. You were like, "Um…oh. Right. Whoops."

CHANGING OR REPEATING YOUR EMOTIONAL HISTORY

Besides the immediate effects that stress h[as], understand how your emotional patterns a[nd] your brain functioning, every minute of th[e] biologist, proved in her groundbreaking bool[k] cell in our body has over a million receptors little docking stations for fear, anger, joy, excite much time "soaking" in one particular emotio stations for that particular feeling, making it e[asier] to experience that feeling again in the future, by default. As cells divide and reproduce, they pay attention to past "needs" and increase the body's ability to repeat the same behavior in the interests of efficiency, such as providing more receptors for fear, *since that's what it thinks you want*. Pretty amazing, huh?

Lest that fact make you feel doomed and depressed, also know our bodies are incredibly resilient in the other direction as well. Science has shown that with deliberate retraining of your emotions, your body will quickly adapt and respond by creating more docks for those newer, positive feelings too. It all comes down to your *intention*.

It's vital for you to manage your stress well for a variety reasons. First, physically, the long-term effects of stress can be extremely damaging: a reduced immune system, increased illness, heart disease, blood pressure, fatigue, memory problems, trouble concentrating, wear and tear on your nervous system, and increased systemic inflammation, which can contribute to a whole host of disorders.

Second, because life is short and you don't want to spend it constantly stressed out. It's not enough to simply *cope* with all the demands that life presents to you. What adventures are you missing out on by keeping your head down and plowing through? What new interests and passions are out there, waiting for you? You want to *enjoy* yourself.

And third, managing and lowering stress will help you with your relationships. How? When you learn how to diffuse strong emotional reactions, you can *respond* to others instead of *react*. This gives you the kind of control you're mistakenly seeking to gain externally.

OVERCOMING YOUR INNER BITCH

The first thing to do when you're overwhelmed by your emotions is *STOP*—and yes, we know, easier said than done. It's tempting to ride the roller coaster of your unpleasant emotions in part because it just feels so damned *familiar*! It may also seem as if you don't have a *choice*. However, if you can begin to deliberately temper your emotional habits, even just a little bit, the simple act of *noticing what's happening*, of bringing your awareness to the fact that you're about to go over the waterfall in a barrel, will begin to steer your inner resources in the right direction.

Assessing your current state, real-time, seems counterintuitive because there's momentum behind your spiraling emotions. Since your logical, problem-solving brain is not in charge, the actions you take now may *feel* better (like replying with a scathing email, because she deserves it!), but be damaging in the long run and only make your situation worse.

When you start to become upset, recognize you need to handle your feelings. Then, depending upon the urgency, choose a self-soothing technique to manage your emotions, from short and simple, to more in-depth and involved. We hope you'll read this chapter while in a good state of mind, so you can truly understand and absorb the stress release techniques we're about to describe. But even if you turn to this section in a crisis, you should still be able to scan through some options and land upon one that will work for you.

QUICK TOOLS FOR CREATING IMMEDIATE RELIEF

In the heat of the moment, when you're at the peak of that emotionally flooded feeling, it may be hard to slow down enough to use some of the more in-depth techniques that follow. So the first thing you want to do is find a way to release and soothe the intense emotions that are bubbling at the surface.

Try your hand at one or more of these calming techniques:

- Put your hand on your stomach and focus on pulling some gentle breaths into your diaphragm that reach your hand. Don't force your breath or you'll end up feeling stressed and dizzy. Remember, gently, gently...

- Imagine breathing in and out through your heart. Your heart has its own wisdom and tuning into it can activate your vagus nerve, which is part of your *relax and recuperate* parasympathetic nervous system.
- Alternatively, hit the stairs at work, take a walk around the block or run in place if you have some privacy.
- Dance to music you love. Music is perfect for tuning into some worn "grooves" in our brains that take us to happy emotional places. Just make sure to avoid dark and brooding and go for the bright and upbeat or funky, bass-laden stuff. This is *not* the time for emo.
- Close your eyes and repeat a mantra in your mind that resonates with you. "I am safe. Everything will be okay. All is well, even though this is hard right now. Nothing lasts forever. This too shall pass."

More information about why these techniques work:

NAME THAT EMOTION

In his book *Just Listen,* Mark Goulston, M.D. says that when we put words to our emotions, the amygdala calms down almost instantly, taking us from "animal survival" mode to "higher brain/thinking and logic" mode. That's because we become the *witness.* We are observing ourselves and our situation from a higher vantage point instead of just being sucked into the situation. It's the difference between *looking* at the dolls in a dollhouse, and being *trapped* in Barbie's penthouse, ready to pull your hair out, if only your plastic hands worked!

In this higher-brain mode, we are able to logically think through a problem to find a solution. We can't get there if we are swimming in the sludge of swamp-like emotions.

DEEP BREATHS

Have you ever tried to think of two things at exactly the same time? It's impossible. That's one of the reasons deep breathing works so well. If you concentrate on your breath, the inhalation and exhalation, you interrupt the thoughts leading to your acute, emotional reaction. With a break in the chain reaction, your body has a chance to return to its resting state where rational thinking and logic come back into focus.

Some people find that taking a deep breath actually stresses them out! It brings their attention to the fact that their breathing is tight and constricted, high up in their chest, instead of lower down into a soft, relaxed belly. If this happens to you, try making your exhale longer than your inhale, pushing out the very last bit of air in your lungs. Over the next few deep breaths, you'll find it's easier to pull fresh air deeper into your tummy and you'll begin to relax.

REPEAT A SOOTHING MANTRA

Mantras can be individualized and address any issue you want. They're phrases you can repeat over and over in your mind, while taking deep breaths to center yourself. There will be times when your heart is racing (perhaps when you know you're going to be face-to-face with someone from the other household), and the only thing that calms you down is knowing it will soon be over and that everything will be okay... eventually. That's an example of a tried and true mantra at work. You used a mantra without realizing it by telling yourself something like, "This has a beginning and an end. I can make it through this and then I'll be okay."

Other examples of great mantras are:

I am at peace.
This too shall pass.
I am safe and protected in this very moment.
It's not about me.
I can handle whatever comes my way.

Mantras work because you're intentionally bringing positivity into your consciousness. Try this quick exercise and repeat after us, "I hate her. She causes me such misery." How did that feel in your body? Did you feel tense? Anxious? Where in your body exactly? Did your heart rate increase? What thoughts came up for you?

Now say, "I am safe no matter what happens. I choose to be at peace," at least ten times, while taking slow, easy deep breaths. Feel the difference? Did you feel more relaxed and settled? What thoughts came up for you?

When we tell ourselves we are comforted, we become comforted. It might take a while to find a mantra that works for you, so keep searching until you do. You'll find an endless supply on the Internet. Don't get discouraged if yours suddenly stops working—sometimes when we repeat the same words over and over, they lose their meaning for us or perhaps our situation is no longer relevant. If this happens, simply find a new one!

PHYSICAL MOVEMENT

You don't have to be a star athlete or yoga goddess to enjoy the de-stressing benefits of being active. Even a small amount of movement will release the "feel-good" neurotransmitters called endorphins. It's virtually impossible to feel extremely stressed when endorphins are pumping through your bloodstream. Is there a sport or physical activity you enjoy? Some of us do better in solitary sports where we can lose our thoughts and just enjoy the feeling of moving our bodies, and some of us crave the communal feeling and camaraderie of team sports.

Don't let some arbitrary ideas about what you "should" look like, what your weight "should" be, and what level of fitness you "should" already have *before you start exercising* (which actually makes no sense!) deter you from using your body. It's *your* body and you have the right to do with it what you will, judgments from others be damned! Will anyone else's critical opinion really make a difference to you, five minutes after they're gone? No!

As women, we're all too used to scanning our bodies and faces with an electron microscope, measuring ourselves against friends, neighbors and impossibly airbrushed freaks of nature from the media and find ourselves lacking. It's up to *us* to change the scripts we're running in our minds. Let's say you're running down the street and your stomach is pooching out or your thighs or butt are jiggling like they have a life of their own. *So what if they are?* Sadly, this is exactly the kind of scenario that keeps us from taking action. Exercise is about *you* and *how you feel*. Don't make someone else's two-second, negative opinion of you more important than the good feelings and de-stressing benefits that exercise can create for you. (Chances are they're not even thinking about you anyway—most of us are all wrapped up in ourselves!) What can you love about yourself? How can you embrace your beautiful body and face—exactly as it is, without changes—right now?

We were all made to move and fully inhabit our own skin. If you have trouble feeling gratitude for your body, *imagine how grateful you'd be to have your current capacities if you suddenly became paralyzed from the neck down.* If nothing else, the humble walk can do wonders for a tight, constricted body and mind. Get out of your environment and outside. If you can't go outside or you only have five minutes at work, walk up and down the stairwell or make an excuse to go to the parking lot.

Your body longs to breathe, to stretch, to take in fresh air, to feel strong again—exactly as it is now. So let it! And give your mind and emotions a break. Your problems with the other woman and the other household are not all there is to *you*.

IN THE WORDS OF OUR READERS

Kacey (mom, stepmom): *"In both roles, I would take some time for me (read a book, spa day, or do a craft that both the children and I enjoy to do together) and after each action of release, I was calmer and more able to evaluate the situation. If I was wrong in any way, I apologized to the other party. If I wasn't, as hard as it was to accept, I had to realize the other party might not ever apologize. As the mom, it took 12 years to receive an apology from my children's stepmom, and it wasn't an apology, but more like an understanding from her that I wasn't as my ex-husband portrayed me. As the stepmom, my husband telling me daily how much he appreciates me and loves me certainly helps."*

S. B. (divorced mom): *"I disengage rather quickly and have a rule of not communicating until 48 hours after a disagreement. This allows me as well as my ex time to cool down. I found that talking about my issues with other bio-moms has really worked. They 'get it,' rather than my friends who are not divorced. Also, it's a unique experience, having your spouse consider you a good* *parent while you're married, but then a bad parent now that we're divorced. It's a tough road that I am learning how to walk down every single day of my life now."*

Leila (stepmom): *"Walking in the woods with my dogs always, always helps."*

Katie P. (stepmom): *"I have a story I tell my stepdaughter when she's upset that also helps me. If someone looked at just an elephant's tail and nothing else, what would someone think an elephant looked like? Probably nothing like a real elephant. So when you are upset about something, just evaluate whether you are looking at the whole elephant or just the elephant's tail."*

L.B. (divorced mom, stepmom): *"What I thought would work: over-explaining myself, such as my current financial situation or the things that are going on in my life right now to give the other household a clearer picture, in the hopes that they would have more understanding. Totally blows up in my face every time or would be used against me at a later date. What works: short and sweet and to the point. When feeling threatened or provoked, I immediately disengage or simply ignore. After I disengage, I find a way to blow it off: get a drink with a friend, buy myself something, cook dinner, work out, etc."*

HEAVY-LIFTING, TRANSFORMATIVE TOOLS

Once you've gotten your amygdala under control, try the following techniques to calm yourself even further. These are meant for use in the moment as well, but can require a little more focus and privacy (but not always). For best results, use them repeatedly over time.

FINDING ACCEPTANCE IN THE PRESENT

Have you ever heard the phrase, "What you resist, persists"? Basically, wherever you're placing your focus is what you will attract in your life.

Three reasons we resist how terrible things *actually are* when you're not getting along with the other woman or the other household:

- You're not used to having anyone actively, blatantly dislike you—everyone else you know seems to like you just fine! It's weird and unnerving.
- You believe if the other side would just understand your viewpoint, they would change their perspective and then their behavior.
- You can't accept that there's a difficult situation in your life that you can't control or fix—there's *got* to be a way to either resolve it or make it go away.

So if you're spending your day complaining about the other woman, mentally reliving the last nasty email she sent you or wondering when the next crappy email will happen—you're just going to attract more of the same. But if you learn how to reduce your resistance to those negative experiences, then you're freer to move on and concentrate on the good and the beauty in your life.

Where many people get tripped up is that amorphous "in-between" space of acceptance and taking action to fix a problem. They're worried that if they accept their current situation, they will suddenly feel deflated and "beaten," like the other party has won. Your subconscious mind fears that you won't be on duty anymore, protecting yourself. But really, acceptance just means acknowledging the reality of your feelings, their impact on you, and seeing the situation for what it is. It doesn't mean, "Well, she's treating me like crap, I'm okay with that." It means saying, "She's treating me like crap, and it makes me feel angry and hurt. It sucks, but there it is. Right now, I can't make the situation go away, no matter how hard I try. Okay, moving on now…"

When you stop resisting your pain, you're more able to release it, a little at a time.

The Bouncing Ball Of The Past And The Future

Another idea to consider about the present moment is how little time you actually spend in it! Picture yourself on a line. The right end of the line is the future. The left end is the past. Theoretically, you're in the middle, in the present. But if you think about it, where is your attention most of the time? To the left, on something that happened this morning, yesterday, last week, even months or years ago? Or does it continually jump around at random points in the future? A few hours from now, this evening. Tomorrow, next week or next month. Next year. Ten years from now? Think of how much time and attention you're giving to things that have already happened or aren't even here yet! When the future comes—*as the present*—you can deal with it then.

Most of us spend way too much time going over repetitive thoughts involving the future that never even come to pass. Thoughts about our jobs, our partnerships, our kids, our homes, families, friendships, bodies, etc. We use fearful thoughts about unwanted scenarios to "motivate" ourselves, but all we end up doing is reinforcing the feeling that something bad is coming our way. Your thoughts are likely bouncing back and forth at light speed. Past. Future. Past, future. Pastfuturepastfuturepas—! If you're constantly jumping around like a ping-pong ball on the line of time, how much time are you spending actually savoring what you have?

If you feel dismayed by your answer, just know you're not alone. Most of us are doing the same thing. Luckily, you only have to take the present in tiny little slices. Because that's all life is. Teeny pieces of time. And most of us are lucky enough to have the luxury of having many more come to us, so let's be grateful and not throw them away like we have an endless supply.

Even if you don't have life all figured out yet, gently guide yourself back into the present. This moment is actually *safer* than what just happened to you because you're *away* from it. And you're protected from the future too, because for now, whatever you're imagining is just an idea *that hasn't happened yet!*

Do Some Guided Journaling

Writing in a journal or diary is an opportunity to explore areas where you're feeling stuck, unsure or challenged. Guided journaling can be a great way to not only release your stressors in a safe and therapeutic manner, it can also help you uncover subconscious thoughts that may be hindering your ability to overcome current challenges and heal past wounds. For best results, make sure you can keep your journal private and secure. Online with a secure password might be a good idea, if you're worried about your physical journal being discovered some day.

GUIDED VISUALIZATION AND MEDITATION

As mentioned earlier in this chapter, our body reacts very similarly whether you're *actually* experiencing something or just thinking about it. That's why emotional stress can be can be so damaging. The good news is it works with positive experiences too. Guided visualization and mediations where you manage the direction of your attention can be used to release emotional and physical stress. Visualize anything from illness leaving your body to being at your favorite vacation spot, stress-free and at peace. This general exercise is also handy if you're at work or can't get away from the family. You can actually just close your eyes for a moment and think of something wonderful. If you're sly, you can even pretend to be reading a book or magazine while visualizing!

The HeartMath Institute has discovered some fascinating research on the native wisdom of the heart, which contains almost as large a store of serotonin as our brain! In their cutting-edge book, *The HeartMath Solution*, the authors describe how the heart is actually the strongest biological oscillator in the human system and has the ability to bring the entire body into resonance or "entrainment" when one deliberately focuses on the feelings of appreciation, compassion, love and forgiveness. You can use the power of your heart to "soak" negative emotions and loosen the hold of dense, long-held fears and upsets, eventually healing them altogether. One exercise can be used in the moment and the other requires 5-10 minutes (we include a variation of it in Chapter 12), but both are highly recommended.

For more information on HeartMath, **see www.heartmath.com**.

MEDITATION

There are various types of meditation. The type we offer in this book consists of repeating a specific mantra, thinking about what the words mean to you, and what you visualize and feel when you repeat them. Each chapter in Section Three, *Making Progress,* offers you multiple mantras to meditate on. Choose one or all of them. Experiment. The choice is yours. Below are basic instructions for you to follow for each meditation:

Sit quietly in a private place where you can relax, without interruptions. Deliberately soften and relax any part of your body that feels tense and tight. Take several deep, easy breaths, releasing any tension you're feeling in your body. Bring your awareness to your heart and let your heart soften and open. You can imagine yourself breathing easily through your heart. Now take one mantra of your choice from the list we have provided in the chapters in Section Three and repeat it silently or aloud.

As you repeat the affirmation, open yourself to the possibility that there is wisdom and truth in it, just waiting for you. You don't have to work hard to absorb this truth or wisdom. Just know the very act of softening and opening to the words will benefit your mind and your emotions.

If you find it hard to sit with the mantra you're working with, you're always free to choose another one that genuinely excites you or gives you a feeling of possibility. If you're still plagued by mental chatter, you can simply focus on generating appreciation for all the good in your life: the people, places and experiences you love; your health; the blessings of sunlight and green grass and beautiful places in nature.

There are additional instructions in each *Making Progress* chapter about doing an even simpler form of meditation with the affirmations when you first wake up in the morning or fall asleep at night. Please see individual chapters for more information.

DO SOME TAPPING

There's a popular, new treatment modality that's proving to be incredibly effective in helping people release negative emotions quickly on a permanent basis. It's called meridian tapping, emotional acupuncture, or Emotional Freedom Technique (EFT). It was popularized by therapist Gary Craig in the 1990s. While strange looking (you tap on certain points on your face, chest, hands and head while repeating certain phrases), it's one of the things that created the most healing for Jennifer in particular.

The idea is to "unclog" certain energy pathways in your body while tapping. You focus on the current stressful situation at hand, give voice to your distressing thoughts, and tap in "rounds" on certain points. As you go around in cycles, you start to feel your negative feelings shift and lighten as you change the language you're using to steer yourself in a positive direction. It's an amazing way to access some of the deep-down, buried stuff of your subconscious and transform your feelings, sometimes in as little as ten minutes. There are free manuals on how to do it online and there is a burgeoning community of practitioners and professionals. Many traditional therapists swear it is one of the fastest methods to relief that they've ever used with their clients.

THE LOWEST OF THE LOWS: WHEN NOTHING WORKS

We want to say a word about those really rough times when no amount of deep breathing, tapping or guided journaling is going to relieve your pain. Because it will happen. We've been there—sobbing uncontrollably in the shower, thinking that we're going to feel this bad forever.

There will be times when you need to release the emotions that have built up, like a pressure valve that's been closed for too long. And what we want to say about those moments is this: it's okay.

Let it out—feel as awful as you need to, but *treat yourself lovingly while you do*. The last thing you need when you're at your lowest point is to beat yourself up for it. Instead, we want you to comfort yourself. Give yourself permission to feel this way. Give yourself love in this moment instead of grief, shame, or guilt. Because once this moment passes (and we promise it will), we don't want you to then have to conquer the shame that accompanied it. The better you can treat yourself during these times, the quicker you will move through them.

When we feel like crap, we often do something to ourselves that makes it ten times worse: *we make ourselves wrong for feeling the way we do in the first place*. We think the fact that we're having a hard time somehow proves that:

- We're screwed up worse than everyone else.
- Everyone else is handling things better than we are.
- We're undeserving of love, compassion or having our needs met.

We feel ashamed that we're upset, so we start from the basis of being wrong from the get-go. It's like taking a shower while standing in mud and wondering why we feel gross. How and why does this happen so easily?

It's complicated. But it's also wonderfully simple.

RUMMAGE AROUND IN THE BASEMENT (OF YOUR SUBCONSCIOUS BELIEFS)

Perhaps your parents ignored you, abused you, or repeatedly told you that you'd never amount to anything. Or maybe they were loving, but so overprotective that deep down inside, you believed you weren't smart enough to do anything well on your own. Whatever your experience, you're likely holding onto some ancient, false beliefs about yourself and they're affecting your relationships today.

Here's a fact we can't believe they don't teach everyone in school: many of the thoughts we think are totally inaccurate. Some of them are even out-and-out lies. Seriously. And still, we would defend some of those thoughts to the death—until—right before you fall asleep at night and the veil between reality and dream-time is at its thinnest. A little bubble of realization gurgles its way to your consciousness and you think, "Oh. Hmmm, yeah... Maybe I was a bit *off* on that one there."

The *last* thing we want to do when things aren't going well is admit we flubbed because admitting we're wrong is all tangled up with our self-worth. If we admit we made a mistake, then that must mean *we* are wrong, personally; deserving of disrespect, scorn, maybe even abandonment. That theory is untrue. But it doesn't keep us from behaving like it is.

If this resistance to the inaccuracy of our thoughts doesn't make any sense, consider the fact we are dealing with thousands of impressions and pieces of input a day. We're doing our best to create and maintain order, predictability, and control. We make assumptions about all kinds of things for the sake of speed and efficiency. After all, who wants to think every time you get into your car: *this is potentially life threatening. I need to prepare for battle!* We think in generalities. We gloss over inconsistencies. If as children, we were told black was white and white was blue, we went ahead and believed it to please our caretakers, even though we may have sensed something wasn't right.

Let's look at this idea in action.

A mom and a stepmom barely know each other in real life, but they're making progress toward creating some kind of working relationship. Then one of them reads a comment that the other has made on Facebook, thinking it was directed at her. She bristles, indignant the other woman is speaking about her online to her friends and family instead of to her face. She feels insulted, betrayed, and exposed.

Let's eavesdrop on her potential thought process:

I can't believe she just did that! All the smiles and saying hello from before, it was all a lie.

And all her friends must think I'm an idiot. Look at how they're laughing at what she said. What a bitchy thing to do. And her friends suck too for not expecting better behavior from her.

I'm never going to trust her again. That's it for me. You get one chance to mess up with me and then that's it. Maybe if she apologizes, I could try again, but if not, forget it. I'm done.

I knew I should have listened to everybody else when it came to playing nice with her. You give her an inch and she takes a mile.

Why didn't I listen to my intuition? I always miss stuff like this. I'm too nice. She's been taking advantage of me all along. I'm such a pushover. Why can't I get my shit together? Well, I'll show her. If she thinks she can walk all over me, she's got another thing coming. The next time she needs me to be extra cooperative or pick up the slack with the kids somehow, good luck. Ain't gonna happen.

Do you see what's happening here? How one thought just slides into another, like a barrel gathering mud going downhill?

The woman above made some big assumptions about the other person's motives, character and what's going to happen in the future. She's even rein-terpreting the past. She's making plans to protect herself from further pain and upset. And she's judging herself harshly as well.

Sounds normal enough, huh? But what if that original Facebook post wasn't directed to her counterpart at all? We'll talk more about the dangers of making assumptions in Chapter 9, Support: Making Progress, but for now, let's look at the situation if the second woman asked for clarification instead of jumping to conclusions. It might go something like this:

Betty, I noticed that post on Facebook. I feel like you and I are working so hard on our relationship and actually getting somewhere, but I couldn't help thinking that maybe you were referring to me in that post. I hope not, but if you are, I'd like to discuss what might have caused you to say that.

The other woman replies with: *Oh my gosh, no! I was referring to my sister-in-law. She can be so difficult sometimes!*

See how differently that went? Conflict averted. Stress released. Relationship intact. Granted, such an over-simplified, picture-perfect outcome isn't always the case, but how many of us are willing to put ourselves out there and ask, just in case it is?

HOW-TO: FIND THE SUBCONSCIOUS MESSAGES INFLUENCING YOUR THOUGHTS AND FEELINGS

Grab a pen and some paper. Find a quiet space where you won't be disturbed for a period of time. Make sure you have the privacy to really feel your feelings. In this exercise, you're going to dip back and forth between feeling, hearing your mental dialogue, and writing down what you are saying inside your head.

At the very end, you're going to bring yourself out of the feeling and back into the present moment, so you can analyze your mental dialogue from a more grounded you. To begin:

1. Focus on one specific event. If you try to tackle a situation with lots of memories of different events, you'll end up overwhelming yourself. Pretend you're watching one short scene, as if it were a ten-second snippet of a movie.
2. Create a simple description of the situation and all of your feelings. Name each of the emotions, as if you were a scientist making notes. You're allowed more than one!

   "This movie would be called, I Can't Believe She Glared at Me That Way. *I feel anger, embarrassment, hurt and confused."*
3. Note where you feel these feelings in your body and write that down.
4. In a stream-of-consciousness way, what phrases come to mind when you complete the following sentences as you re-experience

the previous event? It's okay to be as raw and honest as you want to be. No one is listening to your innermost thoughts but you, and you can always get rid of your notes afterward. You may be shocked to hear yourself say thoughts that are extreme, mean-spirited, self-pitying—things you'd never say out loud in a million years. If you hear stuff like this in your mind, good for you! You're drilling down to the real thoughts that are running your subconscious and you're *making them visible.*

- *She always (behavior):* _____

  _____ (as many phrases as come to mind)
- *That's because she's* _____

  _____ (as many phrases as come to mind)
- *And people, in general are* _____

  _____ (as many phrases as come to mind)
- *Which means I have to then*_____

  _____ (as many phrases as come to mind)
- *Because nothing ever* _____

  _____ (as many phrases as come to mind)
- *Because I'm* _____ _____

  _____ (as many phrases as come to mind)
- *And life is* _____ _____

  _____ (as many phrases as come to mind)
- *Taken altogether, this means my life will always be* _____

  _____ (as many phrases as come to mind)

It's okay if you jump around with your notes, going from statements about her and what's she's like to defensive or negative statements about yourself and the people you love. Just keep writing until you run out of steam.

Now we're going to look at what you're saying to yourself with a more critical, discerning mind.

Take one statement at a time and ask yourself "Is this *always* true? Are there *never* exceptions? Is this statement false? Is it maybe just an I don't know?" Something may "feel" so true and real and absolute that you have a strong resistance to acknowledging any exceptions.

What you will find is that there are some core beliefs buried in there that are not serving you, but you're still acting as if they are set in stone. The real zingers are the ones that you get stuck on—put a star next to those.

Now, create the opposite statement of each zinger and see how it feels to say each one aloud to yourself. Take a deep breath and acknowledge your bravery and hard work.

What choices do you now want to make about how to move forward?

_____

_____

_____

BONUS JOURNAL QUESTION

Do these feeling or issues remind you of anything from your past, no matter how long ago?

_____

_____

IN THE WORDS OF OUR READERS

Kacey (divorced mom): *"This past year the behavior of my ex reminded me of the last year of our marriage. The day he introduced me to his girlfriend (while he was still married), I felt horrible for his wife, my children's stepmom. All the challenges and bumps in the road made me realize maybe she was dealing with the same issues I had during my marriage. That is when I sent my children's stepmom an email letting her know we may not have always agreed over the years, however we did agree on one thing: to love the* *children. Today we are not friends but we are cordial to each other when around the children."*

J.M. (stepmom): *"My ex was a serial cheater (as in more women than you can count on one hand), and I was afraid to leave for a long time. I think if I'd never experienced that blow to my confidence, I wouldn't feel so annoyed by my husband's ex-girlfriend being around. I totally trust my husband, but it's hard to feel that 100% faith in anything once that's happened. It changes a person."*

Zen (divorced mom, former stepmom): *"During our custody case in which the mom eventually conceded, I saw a therapist to help me with the stress of the case. She asked to meet my now ex. After meeting with him once she suggested I read the* Emotionally Unavailable Man. *I thought she was crazy, he was so supportive of me, and so devoted. At a later appointment, another psychologist suggested I read* Toxic Relationship Patterns. *When my ex walked out on me for another woman a few years after that, I thought back to those two therapists and what they were trying to tell me. As a stepmom, it can really help to realize that the patterns experienced in your husband's first marriage may be deeply rooted in the man you love. And that even if he doesn't show that negativity to you, if it is a part of his divorced parent culture with mom, it is very important to examine where that comes from. I do remember thinking, 'I hope they never turn on me that way.' And they did."*

GET GOOD AT THIS STUFF!

It's important to learn how to regularly use at least one or two self-soothing techniques from this chapter. You know how you make a New Year's resolution and then stick to it all year long? Yeah, neither do we. It's easy to find something wonderful that you just *know* will make a positive difference in your life, and then, two weeks later, forget all about it. These tools will only work if you continue to use them. By practicing them routinely, they'll become part of your lifestyle, not just something you do when you *happen* to remember. The key is to *just try* one of them with an "*Okay, whatever. May as well…*" kind of attitude and see what happens! Just like the difference between riding a bike outside in the fresh air and *reading* about riding a bike. It's in the *doing* that you'll finally really *feel* a change for the better in your psyche. And then, next thing you know, you'll find yourself *yearning* for the kind of mental and emotional shift that you know you can get from one or more of these techniques.

Here are some other things to keep in mind about learning new ways to manage your emotions:

- **Using these is like regularly taking out the trash and airing out your house.** You wake up, take a shower, eat breakfast, brush your teeth, get the kids up, go to work, come home and make dinner—you get the idea. We all have patterns to our lives. Our thoughts also have patterns. These *thoughts* generate *emotions and physical responses in our bodies,* which leads to more thoughts. If our thinking is causing us emotional and physical distress, we need to change our thinking and break that pattern. The way to do this is to start a *new* pattern. It takes approximately 30 days for a new behavior to become a habit. By using one or two of the above techniques regularly, you can actually create a habit where you alter long-standing thought patterns from negative to positive.
- **Create reminders to handle problems in the moment**. Until these new coping techniques become second nature, you'll need to be intentional about using your new tools. One way to do this is to set reminders for yourself throughout the day. You can keep a sticky note on the bathroom mirror, set an alarm on your phone to go off three times a day, or wear a bracelet. What kind of reminders have worked for you in the past? What are some other ways to remind yourself of your new mindset?
- **Get support so you can share your insights.** This helps them stick better and makes it easier to change your behavior. Talking about your new insights will help them become ingrained. As an added bonus, you'll likely help others by sharing your own story.
- **Regularly journal your insights to show yourself the progress you're making.** When you're feeling stuck, looking at your

previous insights may be the swift kick in the butt you need to get back on track. It can also be helpful to see how far you've come.

AS WE LEAVE THIS CHAPTER

You can't ignore this chapter and expect anything to change! If you do, it's like saying, "Let's totally clean and reorganize this stuffed-to-the-brim, messy, dusty garage. But let's not take anything out of it! Let's leave the old, moldy stack of newspapers, the mouse poop over there in the corner next to the bag of birdseed with a hole in it, and the gasoline-soaked rags from cleaning up the lawnmower."

It's going to be near impossible, right?

Using these tools, hell—*any* emotional management tools that work for you, means that you can now *respond* instead of *react*. You'll be more likely to let logic take center stage, rather than emotion. Can you imagine how different your interactions would be if you used less emotion when dealing with someone who drives you up a wall?

Instead of reacting with a judgmental tone, hurt feelings, and blame lingering in the air with words you can't take back—you might actually move through the interaction with *minimal damage done*—to both parties. And guess what follows? The *absence* of repetitive internal dialogue about how unfair life is, about how horribly you were treated, about how you let the other person get to you, *again*. You might even be able to move along on your merry way, feeling stronger.

You want more for yourself than just surviving here, right? We certainly want more for you! Now let's apply the tools to the problems.

SECTION THREE
MAKING PROGRESS

CHAPTER 8
INSTINCTS: MAKING PROGRESS
(a messy reality vs. managing our natural reactions)

OPPOSING REFLEXES

In *Chapter One: Instincts*, you learned one of the biggest reasons divorce-connected families are so difficult is that our instincts are working against each other. There are biological expectations within romantic relationships and parent/child relationships that make sense in the context of a nuclear family, but are at odds once you have two, overlapping family units. "Emotional authority" is at work, causing each side to feel as if only *they* can truly see what's in the best interest of the children, even if it's the opposite of what the other side feels and believes.

As you'll see below, all of us are already stressed to varying degrees by the realities of our lives *outside* our families and our threshold for being triggered by dual-family challenges varies at any given moment. Some of us have already reached our breaking point and just want the other side to stop their difficult behavior so that we can catch our breath. We feel desperate and trapped in a vicious cycle of stress and obsession since we are powerless to change the other person or household.

In this chapter, we'll provide you with some tips on how to dissolve the innate feelings of disappointment and resistance you feel with the other household, and put the power to create peace back in your own hands. We'll help you find compassion for yourself and the suffering you've been experiencing, even for the people you've been traditionally seeing as adversaries.

Lastly, we'll end with a meditation to help you feel calmer during a cycle of conflict. Choose to rise above these challenges and reduce their negative impact on you and your family. You can do it!

THE ELEPHANT IN THE ROOM

One thing that's hard to get people to understand if they're not in a dual-household (or more!) situation is how incredibly difficult it is to have the other woman, the other family, *present* in your daily life. When a romantic couple without children splits up, that's generally it. You go your separate ways with separate lives, separate homes, and often separate sets of friends and family. You're done. And you're glad!

Not in these set-ups, as you already know all too well.

Now the other woman in your life is like an infiltrator, an invader, constantly trumping decisions and milestones that should be rightfully *yours*. She's there in the way you have to schedule your days, your weeks, and your *year*. She's there in the children's behavior, maybe even visible in their facial features. She's there in your ex's new stance on a subject that used to not be a problem. It feels like nothing is *yours* anymore.

So let's take a look at the impact she's *really* having on your life. To what extent are you struggling with the reality that an unwanted stranger has a starring role in how the months play out?

If you were to examine each of the areas below, how would you rate your satisfaction in each area? What is the level of conflict you are experiencing with her and the other household? How would you rate your feelings of power and control? The level of hope you have for things getting any better?

Rather than make you write out a lot of details, let's have a little fun. Grab a pen or pencil or even some colorful markers or crayons.

EXERCISE—HER LOUSY IMPACT ON MY LIFE

For each item below, fill in the box to rate your current level of stress or satisfaction, as far as the other woman's influence upon that area of your life. Shade each box with a pen or pencil, starting from left to right. The further left your shading, the lower the amount for you. The further right your shading, the stronger you agree.

Life Area	Amount of active conflict	Feeling of power and control	Hope for future improvement	Overall Satisfaction
Romantic Partnership				
Bonds with the Children				
Parenting or Step-Parenting				
Communication				
Scheduling				
Finances				
Legal Issues				
Extended Family				
Friendships				
Work				
Household decisions				

Even though it might freak you out a bit to see the "negative" boxes filled in and the "positive" boxes looking pretty lonely, we also want you to take note of the areas of your life where you're actually doing okay. Make a mental note of those topics. It's likely that you're already playing to your strengths there. Take a moment to acknowledge yourself for that, right now.

JOURNAL QUESTIONS: HER EMOTIONAL IMPACT AND WHAT I'M DOING WELL

Where do most of my challenges seem to lie? What do I think about that?

_____
_____
_____

What am I handling well? Where have I grown and made progress?

_____
_____
_____

I acknowledge myself for:

_____
_____
_____

OTHER BURDENS YOU'RE CARRYING

In hearing hundreds of stories from moms and stepmoms about how horrible the other person is, we sometimes wish we could ask them: is it really *just* her or is there *something else* contributing to your unhappiness? We're loathe to admit when this might be the case, because that doesn't make for such a clear, succinct (or entertaining) story.

Other sources of stress shape the way you feel about the other woman and your inability to cope. If you're in bed with the flu and you can barely focus, your threshold for conflict is going to be much lower than if you're feeling healthy. Sometimes our lowered tolerance isn't even that obvious. Maybe you're still hitting the gym four times a week and having a weekly date night with your husband, but the cumulative pressures have finally caught up with you and all you need is one. more. thing. to push you over the edge.

Remember, this book is about you taking control of your life, whether she decides to change or not. Let's make sure you have a complete inventory of your stressors so you know exactly what's "yours" and what is related to her or the other household

IN THE WORDS OF OUR READERS

Katie P. (stepmom): *"Oh man. I was a monster leading up to our wedding. She couldn't do anything right. I was so afraid that she'd try to impose on our big day that I jumped to being a crazy lady any time I felt even just a little bit threatened by her. My low point was when she told my stepdaughter not to curl her hair. I* snapped *and sent her a slew of nasty text messages from, 'You don't know how to do your daughter's hair!' (which isn't really true) to how our wedding plans had nothing to do with her and how she felt. Not one of my finest moments."*

Tori (divorced mom, stepmom): *"When my oldest daughter's antics reached what I stupidly then thought was the peak, my ex-husband and I decided she would go live with him. It happened to be the same time that my husband's ex-wife was visiting my stepson and was being all possessive. I was mad at my daughter, furious that her stepmom was refusing to meet me even though my daughter was going to go live with her, and feeling like a crappy mother all around. I took out my frustration on my stepchild's mom. I posted stupid, hurtful things about moms who abandon their children, told her how much she sucked because she couldn't handle the boys for even one overnight visit (she hadn't lived with* *them in two years). I told her how much happier the boys were with my husband and I. Honestly, my behavior had to do with me feeling like a failure as a mom and had nothing to do with my stepchild's mom. I'm not proud of it, although we both laugh now at how awful we were to each other that week and didn't even meet face-to-face for another six months."*

J.M. (stepmom): *"I don't have enough interaction with her to take anything out on her, but I am guilty of taking things out on my husband. As in, if I am already upset with him and something comes up regarding her, I am mentally thinking, 'Oh, you brought her crap into my life!' She exacerbates whatever is going on in my mind. Not good of me at all."*

When the other person's behavior continually sends you into over-drive you have lost control of yourself. That means there's a good chance something else (or something old) has been provoked. Here's the problem with that: blame the wrong thing and your problems will remain an enigmatic and seemingly impossible source of frustration. Handle the right thing and watch problems with the other household fade away into something manageable or maybe, just maybe, even something *good.*

So let's get down to the nitty-gritty here: how much of your stress is from her and how much is generated by other issues? Complete the exercise below to get an idea of how fulfilled you are in various aspects of your life.

EXERCISE—ALL THE REST OF IT

Rate your fulfillment in all areas of your life. On a 1-5 scale, a 1 means you're fairly miserable in that area in your life and a 5 means it's all shiny and almost perfect.

Look at each issue **independent of her influence** and focus only on how you think you're doing handling each one. After you've rated the following areas, notice what areas could use improving. Make sure to fill out each row of boxes.

Health and Fitness	Family Connected-ness	Parenting relationships	Romantic partnership	Work	Support System	Income vs. Debts
1 2 3 4 5	1 2 3 4 5	1 2 3 4 5	1 2 3 4 5	1 2 3 4 5	1 2 3 4 5	1 2 3 4 5

Self-Care and Nurturing	Confidence & empowerment	Old emotional issues	Fun and Novelty	Learning and Growth	Creativity	Hobbies and Interests
1 2 3 4 5	1 2 3 4 5	1 2 3 4 5	1 2 3 4 5	1 2 3 4 5	1 2 3 4 5	1 2 3 4 5

Humbled? It can be tough to see all the loose ends of your life, wrapped up in neat little boxes. For most of us, seeing all this evidence that we're not "doing it right" or *doing enough* is too uncomfortable to face for even a minute, let alone having a permanent record of it in a book!

But rest assured, our aim is to help you feel a whole lot better about what you *can* do and to show you how to do more of it. No one ever gets to have absolute satisfaction in *all* areas of their life anyway, unless they're dead. And you're not. So be happy about *that!*

NOW HELP ME FEEL BETTER

Here's the bottom line: it's often the dynamic *between the two families* that makes your divorced family and stepfamily life so difficult, not necessarily problems you have on a personal level. Of course, it's vital for you to be absolutely honest with yourself about how you're contributing to conflict too. After all, most of our prickly behavior comes from wanting to protect ourselves and those we love from harm. Nevertheless, you must step back and recognize how other stressors in your life are temporarily increasing your sensitivity to and intolerance for conflict, and how they impact your ability to cope.

So keep in mind:

YOUR PROBLEMS ARE LARGELY CREATED BY COMPETING INSTINCTS

These dueling instincts make it difficult for love to flow unimpeded in your family and in hers. You likely feel resistance toward yourself and others for having these problems—and so does she. You are both struggling and fumbling your way through the dark. Acknowledge the negativity of your situation and your resistance to it. Allow yourself your feelings. Remind yourself that it's the nature of the beast. The reason you find this situation challenging is not due to a personal fault or flaw.

Looking back on the Emotional Givens exercise in Chapter 1, what possible truths of yours and hers do you now see differently? How so?

_____

_____

_____

HAVE COMPASSION FOR YOURSELF AND OTHERS

A great place to begin—have compassion for yourself, for even struggling in the first place. One of the ways that we get ourselves all contorted in a sort of emotional version of Houdini's straitjacket is *we reject ourselves* for being upset about our dual family problems.

Home is supposed to be a place where you retreat from the world, where you relax, regroup and recharge. But when home and family become some of the *most contentious aspects* of your life, it's easy to feel like you're failing or, even worse, that *you* personally are a loser because you're having a hard time. When you have this "double negative," your thoughts and feelings get all tangled up and you can't create any forward movement. Realize that you are not alone. The majority of people in your position as a divorced mother or stepmom (or both) are also struggling with instinctive behavior that is clashing against the other person's.

In what ways would you be sympathetic toward a friend who was struggling with the same situation that you're in now? How would you want to nurture them and reassure them? How can you do that with yourself?

_____

_____

_____

SHE'S HUMAN AND HAS HER OWN TRUTH AND PERSPECTIVE

These situations are tough for everyone—she may be suffering just as much as you or other members of your family are. Her own beliefs are driving her behavior and even if she's in the small percentage of women with a personality disorder or mental illness, her beliefs are still 100 percent true in her mind. Your "truth" seems just as illogical to her as hers does to you! Both of you have the right to your own interpretations of reality, no matter how widely they differ.

What truth could she could be coming from? What do you think her strongest beliefs are? (Look back to Chapter One.) How can you allow her the space for her reality and stop trying to change her or "win" against her? What perspective can you take that helps you to feel calmer?

_____

_____

_____

GET A WIDER VIEW OF YOUR LIFE AND READJUST YOUR VIEW OF THE OTHER STRESSORS

It's okay that you're perpetually falling short in one or several areas of your life—it's called _being human!_ While we're all works in progress, it can be tough to keep the progress we have made in mind. The to-do list is always going to be a mile high and yet we often let it, and guilt, run the show. Where we _choose_ to focus our attention is up to us and determines how well we feel like we are doing overall, though that's easy to forget.

In what areas of your life do you feel like you are making progress? What problems have you eliminated recently?

_____

_____

_____

CHECK YOUR THINKING

ROTTEN SEEDS DON'T BLOOM

For this particular topic, *instincts*, it's likely that your thinking is falling along certain repetitive lines. Most of our thoughts pass by so quickly that we don't even realize we're thinking them, much less catch how wildly exaggerated they are. If we saw someone whispering extremely negative, self-defeating thoughts into a friend's ear and witnessed our friend believing these statements and feeling terrible as a result, we'd put an immediate stop to it!

Sadly, we let our patently false thoughts fill up a substantial part of our mental diet because most of us are not used to questioning our own thinking. Our egos would have us believe we *always* know what we're doing, which is not true. *We* are not our egos alone. We are so much more than that.

To help you catch what you might be whispering to yourself, we've listed the most common negative beliefs that may be operating in the background of your thinking. Remember, your beliefs are not *absolute* truth or reality. They are simply beliefs that you have chosen to see as such.

Do any of these negative thoughts below sound familiar? If so, don't despair. We offer some contrasting positive beliefs in our *Affirmations* section that you can adopt to gradually change your thinking and calm your emotions. (Hints on how to implement these follow.)

POTENTIAL NEGATIVE BELIEFS

Here are some examples of negative beliefs you might not realize you have. Put a checkmark next to any you can relate to:

- I can't make a healthy family work because my own family life was too screwed up.

- This is going to fail too.
- I'll never really belong anywhere.
- If one family is happy, then the other one is automatically going to be miserable.
- I feel like an outsider and everyone else has it together.
- I should be able to make it work with my ___ (fill in the blank with a family member).
- It's just not fair that I'm in this situation.
- I have it harder than anyone else.
- I am constantly going to be hurt, no matter what.
- The other household is ruining my child or stepchild's life and/or future.
- The other household is trying to sabotage my parenting/ stepparenting *and* my marriage.
- People are hurting me or pissing me off on purpose.

What are your thoughts about what you checked off?

_____

_____

_____

WATERING THE SEEDS OF HAPPINESS

ACCESSING YOUR SUBCONSCIOUS—TWICE A DAY

Contrary to outdated opinion, we actually *can* reshape long-standing, subconscious beliefs. Repeat the affirmations (listed below) to yourself during times of extra stress or, for best results, for a week or two upon rising or falling asleep. During those two times in particular, you are in a theta brain state and your subconscious mind is at its most impressionable.

Just as our blind, negative thoughts have the power to make us totally miserable, positive thoughts can cause us to feel a sense of hope, possibility and lightness—even if the actual facts of our situation remain exactly the same. Now *that's* a miracle cure!

As we talked about in the Power Tools section, many of our conscious beliefs actually come from subconscious beliefs that became part of our "instructions for life" when we were very young (typically less than five or six years old). Rather than seeing yourself as doomed because subconscious beliefs seem so elusive and difficult to reshape, you might be excited to know that science is continually reaffirming our ability to reprogram our beliefs.

You have two opportune moments every day to input new, more empowering beliefs into your brain: when you wake up and are still a bit sleepy, and right before you drift off into Dreamland at night. This is when you are in a theta state and your subconscious mind is at its most impressionable.

POTENTIAL POSITIVE BELIEFS

Repeat one of the following affirmations to yourself for a week or two upon rising or falling asleep—or during times of extra stress:

- The more people that love the kids, the better.
- I can create a family that works.
- We create new family memories together.
- It's okay for a loving family to make mistakes.
- Everyone is doing the best they can.
- I am okay with not understanding others.
- I easily manage my emotions.
- I learn from my mistakes.
- I allow others to learn in their own way.
- It is not my job to fix anyone.
- I meet my challenges with grace.
- I have compassion for all.

MEDITATION: HAVE COMPASSION FOR A DIFFICULT SITUATION

Follow the steps listed in Section Two for getting yourself into a nice, relaxed state for meditation, then silently repeat the following mantras. Take as much time as you need and sit with the thoughts that come up for you. If you find yourself drifting off into a state of "argument" with the statements below, gently refocus your attention. You may find it's difficult to accept some of these thoughts since your actual day-to-day experience does not match. Try to allow yourself room to ease into them as a potential reality awaiting you in the near future.

See if you can find feelings of kindness and compassion in your heart as you make your way through an inherently challenging family situation. Know that even though you have made mistakes and behaved from a reactive place, you did so from a place of love, with the best of intentions. Forgive yourself for choices you may have made in the moment that did not serve you or your family. Imagine the slate being wiped clean. The past has been erased and you are now free to move on, coming back into the present moment, starting anew. You acknowledge you are human and are still learning.

WORDS TO MEDITATE ON:

I accept this present moment.
I allow my resistance to what is to melt away.
May I have compassion for myself and others.
May I have patience for the things I do not understand.
I accept that we all want to avoid suffering and find happiness.
I forgive myself for my mistakes.
I begin again with a clean slate.
My family is safe and protected.
My home is a refuge of peace and safety.
I allow myself to have peace and happiness.
I trust myself to handle whatever comes my way.
I allow my instincts to guide me with love.
At this very moment all is well.

CHAPTER 9

SUPPORT: MAKING PROGRESS
(validation from others vs. your own higher wisdom)

WHAT HEALTHY SUPPORT LOOKS LIKE

In the *No One's the Bitch* (NOTB) community, many people report that it's hearing from the perspective of "the other woman" that has most opened their eyes and helped them let go of their anger, resentment, hurt, and fear. They hear opinions that they might never have considered had they listened to their regular sources of input and support. Don't get us wrong. We're not saying that a different perspective justifies bad behavior, but it can bring you a new level of understanding and clarity that helps you let go of damaging emotions.

When you're forced to interact with someone who has a high-conflict personality, you have a much better chance of successfully thriving if you look at how you can better protect yourself, instead of wishing and hoping *they* will one day change. Placing the responsibility for your behavior and emotions on your own shoulders puts *you* back in control, instead of perpetuating feelings of helplessness and hopelessness.

If you want to make it through the challenges of your dual-family situation with your sanity intact, you'll need good friends who will tell you the truth, even when you don't want to hear it. Friends and family who will put themselves in the uncomfortable position of potentially making you angry, hurting your feelings, wounding your pride, or eliciting a bad reaction with that honesty. In doing so, they're taking a risk, but ultimately you can trust that their actions come from love and not ego, competition, or wanting to rub your nose in your mistakes. We intuitively know the difference.

Below are some things to keep in mind when seeking support.

People to surround yourself with:

- **Others who have been in your shoes, achieved peace, and handled the situation well.** These are comrades who have been where you are and have managed to create stability. They're not still actively fighting with the other household. They've found a way to live *in* their situation but not let it take over their life.
- **Others who realize your end goal is positivity and not to just continually complain.** Surround yourself with those who support your higher-self goals and won't keep fueling the fire. These people will say, "I see you're really making an effort here. Even though it's tough and there's still conflict, you're doing a great job."
- **Friends who will let you voice your frustrations and then help you look for answers.** They'll say, "Let's brainstorm some potential solutions. What are some other options here?" They understand the initial need to vent, but also know that the end goal is to resolve conflict, even if it's simply within *yourself.*
- **Those who will be truthful with you.** They will call you out on your constant complaining and lack of focus on moving forward. These folks will say, "Actually, I think you might have been out of line there. What you did would have made *me* mad too," or "I hear you focusing all your anger on her, but I don't hear you taking any responsibility here."

A WORD ABOUT FAMILY

Family can be a great support system, but your stress can also weigh heavily on them. It's difficult for them to see how much pain you're in. They want you to feel better *now*. They want you to be "right." They want you to "win." And although these are sweet sentiments, they're not necessarily going to bring you peace and they're certainly not objective. Family is also likely to hold your complaints against the other party. What if one day you work it out? It might be much harder for *them* to forgive than for you. We're not saying don't *ever* turn to family for support. We're just asking you to consider the potential consequences and be judicious with what you share.

A WORD ABOUT MEN

Complaining to men typically doesn't make them change; it just makes them feel bad about themselves, which can lead to distance between the two of you. For stepmoms, complaining to your husband about his ex-wife is likely going to stir up feelings of failure in him. When he sees that you're *not* happy due to *his* situation, he may shut down. For stepdads, he'll want to be the main man in your life. Even though the kids may not be "his," it's important that he feels like he can create coherence and harmony in the house. When he consistently fails to achieve this, it could lead to distance from you and the kids too. Do your best to find a source of additional support elsewhere, and you'll be more able to nurture your marriage, instead of adding stress to it.

THE BENEFITS OF A HEALTHY, TRUTH-TELLING SUPPORT SYSTEM

Are you starting to see how it's in your best interests to not only vent with care, but choose the feedback you trust with discernment as well? Are you beginning to wonder "How can I create this for myself?" The answer is balanced support that's based on honesty and compassion. That kind of support gives you some wonderful gifts. It:

- helps you illuminate your blind spots and see the big picture
- helps you tell the truth about your unhelpful actions and why you might have behaved this way—you can then do the same for her behavior, which depersonalizes it and makes it feel less threatening
- is shorter, quicker, and more powerful than the long stories involved in being a victim
- makes it easier to forgive yourself and forgive others

IN THE WORDS OF OUR READERS

Renee S. (stepmom): *"I definitely sought commiseration at first, which left me wallowing in anger and self-pity. Now I surround myself with wise women who ask me tough questions and keep me honest. It's improved not only my familial relationships, but my overall state of mind as well."*

Holly O. (divorced mom): *"I have learned over the years to not seek support from my family. I think it does my children a disservice to have one side of their family not like their other family. I intentionally seek out women who will challenge me to think about where the stepmom could be operating from emotionally and if that truly impacts the kids, versus me just not liking her actions and words. Hearing the stepmom point of view from others has become of much more importance than having my own feelings validated. Additionally, I no longer avoid speaking of my blended family in therapy. I embrace the fact it has had a huge impact on my life, the good and bad. It was hard to admit I could use some professional help in coping."*

Meagan E. (stepmom): *"I am definitely more open to hearing other sides now than I was before. It doesn't always mean that I will take their advice, but I do seek it out and consider all sides before reaching a decision. Seeking the opinions of both stepmoms and mamas has made me much more even-tempered. It has also made me think more before I throw in my two cents about someone else's problem."*

WEEDING OUT INEFFECTUAL SUPPORT

Which part of your support system isn't working for you? Do you have people in your life who are draining your energy instead of helping to replenish it? Perhaps it's time to do some weeding. Sometimes you have to get rid of what's not working in order to make room for what will.

Throughout your life, people will come and go and new situations will arise. Refer back to the "Rate Your Different Sources of Validation" exercise in Chapter 2 and determine which aspects are negatively influencing you. Take a look at the list below. Do any of these general archetypes below sound familiar to you?

- **Negative and Rigid:** people who are "stuck" in their situation and remain in the "doomed" mindset, thinking the same automatically applies to you
- **Debbie Downers:** people who immediately counteract every positive point you make with a negative one
- **Buck-up:** people who encourage you to be tougher and "Just deal with it," even admonishing you with, "Well, you knew what you were getting into…"
- **Yes Men and Women:** people who don't offer any solutions, but just validate your complaints
- **Geniuses:** people who argue against your experience and try to convince you that you must be wrong and their view is superior
- **Subtle Geniuses:** people who keep wanting to tell you their story to gradually lead you to the blinding realization that you're wrong

Once you've pinpointed these roadblocks in your support system, think seriously about removing them. Not necessarily out of your life, but out of your advice circle. Perhaps you have a friend who's better off being your go-to girl when you need a new pair of shoes, but not objective, sound feedback? Maybe another friend is great to talk to about parenting challenges, such as a baby who's not sleeping through the night or playground battles, but not the stuff that's too close to your heart?

HOW-TO: RESTORE YOUR BALANCE
WHEN YOU NEED SUPPORT

The next time you're faced with an onerous situation and you're about to lose your temper or your eyes are so puffy from crying that you're afraid you're going to bump into the kitchen counter or accidentally run someone off the road, take a run through the following questions to regain your composure.

Take out a separate piece of paper and use these questions below to catch your breath, sort through your thoughts, and create emotional and physical coherence.

- How are you feeling right now? Which emotions are the strongest? (You may have several and they might seem contradictory.)
- Where do you feel these feelings in your body?
- How would you rate your level of discomfort on a scale of 1-10, with 10 being almost unbearable?
- Do you feel the need to *discharge* some of that negativity first, before you'll be open to feedback from a friend? Or do you feel the need to *connect* with another living soul more?
- If you need to discharge energy first, what are some harmless ways to do that? Physical activity? A letter you never send? Accomplishing some simple, unrelated goals? (See also Section Two, Power Tools, for more ideas.)
- If you'd rather connect with a friend or family member:
  * Do you feel a sense of open-ended curiosity? Are you willing to consider the possibilities of a different perspective? That things may not be quite what they seem?
  * Or do you want a sympathetic audience who won't challenge your version of events? Are you tempted to find a solution that "makes everyone happy"? Are your ideas for relief motivated by wanting to feel superior or like the proven victim?
- Rather than making something definitive and concrete happen, do you need to leave yourself some space to come up with a great solution later, when you're in a more grounded state of mind?
- What do you need to hear right now that would truly make you feel better? Can you provide this reassurance for yourself somehow?

Now that you've spent some time considering a wider range of possibilities for your situation, take a few moments to tune into your higher wisdom and see if it has any advice to offer you. Take a few deep breaths and tune into your heart. Then answer the questions below.

JOURNAL QUESTIONS:
ASSESSING THE SUPPORT I NEED RIGHT NOW

What did your heart have to offer you? What did you discover as you answered these questions above? In what ways do you feel better now? Do you still feel the need for new support and a new perspective? What steps can you take to get this?

_____

_____

_____

RETRAINING YOUR BRAIN

Look back at the quiz in Chapter Two called "Oops, I Guess I Did it Again." If you scored a 25–40, there are things you're doing to make your situation worse. It's time to change some of those unhealthy behaviors and catch yourself in the act. There are two tactics you could try instead of the same, old, public song of woe: telling fewer people about a difficult experience or sticking to a shorter, more factual explanation about the event.

For example, the first behavior on the quiz checklist is, "Repeating the most inflammatory parts to a number of people."

MUM'S THE WORD

The more you tell your story to others, the more it gets ingrained in your brain. The more you think about it, the more it physically and emotionally affects you, and the more you keep sharing it with people. It's a nasty cycle that will keep you mired in drama. The next time you're faced with a situation where you'd normally tell a bunch of people how you've been wronged, try doing this instead: share what happened and your feelings about it with only one person. Choose someone you would consider an "effective" support person and then see how long you can go without talking about the incident with anyone else.

JUST THE FACTS, MA'AM

Just like it sounds, when you're sharing an incident, you only share the facts. Leave out any opinions, feelings, insults, judgments or assumptions. If the opportunity comes up (for example, a friend asks you how things are going with the other woman or household) don't indulge in all the nasty details. Use phrases like, "Same ol' same ol'" or "Just the usual…" Below is an example of sharing the typically gossipy way and then using this method:

The usual way: *"Oh, you won't believe what she did. She had the gall to email me and tell me that my child was home sick and vomiting and that she thought it was something I had given her to eat. Can you believe that crap? Who does she think she is? I couldn't believe she was blaming me! The nerve of some people. Like she's Mary friggin' Poppins or something. I told her that this was between me and my ex and that I didn't need her giving me her opinion about my own child. When will that idiot ever learn?"*

Just the facts, ma'am: *"I received an email from my child's stepmom letting me know that my daughter is home sick today. She thought it might have been something I fed her last night."*

Can you see how one evokes all this emotion and other is just, well, almost boring? This is a challenging exercise because without all the commentary, it's more difficult to get your friends on your side. Yet it also helps keep you in a healthier mindset, which is why you're reading this book in the first place, right? It's up to you how you choose to handle these situations. The first method potentially sabotages you and your well-being. The second keeps you present and responsible, out of the emotional muck.

Now that you're armed with some new tools to surround yourself with a more effective support circle, we hope you'll be brave enough to consider new facts and possibilities for long-term challenges you've been struggling with. How have you been misinterpreting the motives of other people? How do you think they might be misinterpreting yours?

CHECK YOUR THINKING

Potential Negative Beliefs

Here are some examples of negative beliefs you might not realize you have. Put a checkmark next to any you can relate to:

- My friends will be mad at me if I change.
- If I stop venting to my friends, we'll have nothing to bond over.
- If I seek out "truth-tellers," they may say something I can't handle.
- I'm right and she's wrong and anyone who can't see that is crazy.
- If I don't gossip, I'll seem too serious and boring.
- I'm embarrassed about "taking the high road." I don't want to seem like a snob to my friends.
- Now I *have to* follow the other person's advice or else I'm a coward or lazy.
- It's better to just try and figure everything out by myself.
- Honestly, you can't really trust anyone. Who knows what secret agenda they have?

What are your thoughts about what you checked off?

_____

_____

_____

INCREASING YOUR POSITIVE BELIEFS

It's possible to dramatically improve the quality of your life by deliberately increasing the number of affirming beliefs "automatically" available to your conscious and unconscious mind. Use the following mantras or affirmations on a daily basis, inputting them into your subconscious twice a day or during a focused meditation. Your choice!

ACCESSING YOUR SUBCONSCIOUS—TWICE A DAY

Contrary to outdated opinion, we actually can reshape long-standing, subconscious beliefs. Repeat the affirmations (listed below) to yourself during times of extra stress or, for best results, for a week or two upon rising or falling asleep. During those two times in particular, you are in a theta brain state and your subconscious mind is at its most impressionable.

MEDITATION: FEELING GOOD IN YOUR OWN SKIN

Follow the steps listed for Meditation in Section Two, Power Tools, and guide yourself into a nice, relaxed state. Then silently repeat any of the following mantras below. Take as much time as you need and let any other thoughts you have float by and fade away. If you find yourself drifting off into a state of "argument" with an affirmation, gently refocus your attention, return to the statement and enhance feelings of softness, warmth and expansion in your heart. Continue until you feel better.

POTENTIAL POSITIVE BELIEFS

Choose two or three that resonate with you and mentally repeat each one, as you breathe slowly and deeply.

- I am open to hearing new perspectives.
- I create my own personal security.
- I remain grounded while hearing challenging feedback.
- I trust myself to make wise, mature decisions.
- I choose to remain calm.
- I welcome a positive resolution for all.
- I release the need to be the victim or prove my position.
- I trust the universe/God (choose language that works for you) to provide me with loving lessons.
- Everything is happening exactly as it should.
- I am safe in this moment.

- I trust my friends and family to help me achieve peace.
- I am capable of creating solutions that work.
- I am growing in maturity and grace.
- I can relax even while I am creating change.
- I don't have to do it all alone.
- It feels good to have a community of support.

CHAPTER 10
MEN: MAKING PROGRESS
(conflicting loyalties vs. clear priorities)

THE TRIANGLE OF LOYALTY AND OBLIGATIONS

There is so much to say about our relationships with men and the dynamic of the man in the middle that we could write an entirely new book about it. (In fact, that's the book Jenna plans to write next.) As a result, what we're covering in this chapter is just the tip of the iceberg.

In Chapter 3, you heard Mario Korf (Jenna's husband) speaking directly to the other divorced and remarried dads out there (we were eager to eavesdrop too!) about his life as a remarried father. Many men seem like such unfathomable mysteries to women. *We're* used to guessing at everyone's potential motives and feelings, but it's so much better to hear about how men think from a man himself, with Mario letting us in on how many dads experience the complex dynamics between two households.

Divorced dads are inhabiting three very different roles at the same time, like a comedian with three separate sections of an audience. Trying to make everyone laugh at the same time is tough going. You try playing to these different groups listed below!

- his children
- his new wife
- his ex-wife

A remarried dad can easily feel like he's caught in the middle of an intricate series of competing demands. Most men don't like to admit that they're not up to the task of carrying an extremely heavy load without complaint, but as we'll see here, it's helpful to take a conscious look at what each party is expecting of him and why he feels pulled in so many conflicting directions.

After a marriage breaks up and a father remarries, *everything* changes when it comes to parenting and partnership. Mothers and fathers may have very different ideas about how communication should occur. How the hands-on details of daily life should be handled (and by whom). How the children should be nurtured and disciplined. How both parties *should* manage difficult emotions in order to successfully parent the children.

Add a new parental figure into this mix and you will often have trouble. To simplify, we're going to focus on the combination of the two parents and the stepmother in this chapter.

In The Words Of Our Readers

Jenny P. (divorced mom/stepmom): *"I attempted to set boundaries in the beginning, only to be regarded as jealous and controlling. If you know me at all, you would know I am typically neither. However, looking back at the way I handled it and really thinking deeper into how I was feeling, I actually* was *jealous! Not of my ex finding someone new, I was quite happy for him. We had been apart for some time and I had long since moved on. I was jealous of my daughter's relationship with another mother figure. Honestly, it was when I faced these fears that I was taken more seriously by my daughter's father and stepmother. It was a change in our relationship (which took years of work) that made all the difference."*

J.W. (stepmom): *"When I started dating my now husband, he almost immediately started including me in decisions about his kids. He always considered me a 'partner' and so my thoughts and feelings mattered to him. I don't think it affected his relationship with his ex at all, because she had no way of knowing I was an integral part of his opinion. He and I would discuss it, we would* *come to a decision, and with that in mind he would talk to his ex and they would work something out. That's not to say I always felt right taking part in those decisions. In the beginning, I contributed less, but as the kids became a part of what I defined as my family and they started to affect my life more, I felt more comfortable in that role."*

Brynn (divorced mom/stepmom): *"When my ex-husband started dating his now-wife, it changed a lot and I wasn't very open to it. We'd had a co-parenting relationship for 10 years that was working. Then, all of a sudden, there was a priority shift that I took really personally and there was this other person (with another opinion) in the picture who I didn't get to have a background check on. I had to just trust my ex-husband's choice and deal with it. It was hard, but I learned."*

Holly O. (divorced mom): *"He met the stepmom shortly after we split and it complicated our relationship, but not in how you would normally think. He became very secretive, not telling me her name, refusing to tell me where she lived. Which is fine if you're not taking my children to her house, but he was. It opened my eyes to the type of person he really was. I realize now why he did this (to have her better believe his story regarding me, and to keep me from potentially telling her about the real reasons we split). Him acting this way made me much more hesitant to send the kids off with him and suspicious of both of them."*

PARENTING AND PARTNERSHIP

Disagreements over parenting and partnership are two of the most contentious issues between parents and between a remarried father and his wife. We all have strong opinions about the best way to raise children that are frequently a carry-over (or a reaction to) the way we were raised ourselves. Our own emotional wounds and memories inform our thoughts and feelings about the way we think things "should be done." Two ongoing mysteries women continually struggle with when it comes to men are how they show us they care (about us and others) and how closely they're paying attention to the things *we* think matter. Let's take a closer look.

HOW MEN SHOW LOVE

Moms thinking they know how men should "be" with their kids starts early. From the moment a child is born, a mother often begins imagining how a child's relationship should unfold emotionally with his or her father. She may hover over him while he's changing a diaper to make sure he's doing it "right," make suggestions about how he holds and plays with the baby, and push him to be expressive with the kids in a way that *she* would be as a loving parent.

Stepmoms may form their own opinions about a father and his relationship with his kids when she and her partner begin dating. How close does he seem to be? How demonstrative? How affectionate? In the back of her mind, she may begin plotting how to "fix" the relationships he has with his children, if she can imagine herself relating to them differently as a parent. It's all too easy for stepmoms to meddle if she thinks dad's not doing enough.

But as author Alison Armstrong loves to say, *"Men are not hairy women!"* If you read Mario's chapter directed at the dads, you may remember him talking about how he relates to his kids, deliberately "hands-off" instead of micro-managing them, letting them learn from their mistakes.

Many women, both moms and stepmoms alike, expect men to show that they love their children the same way a woman would: by asking questions, tending to needs and desires before they're even expressed, and by completing the endless, daily household tasks that signal to the people you love that you're paying attention. However, men may be focused on teaching their children more values-oriented life skills, such as self-discipline (how to accept authority and work hard), integrity (keeping your word and sticking to agreements), and honor (doing the *right* thing regardless of how you feel about it). This broader approach doesn't mean they love their children any less, though it might seem like it to us.

IN THE WORDS OF OUR READERS

Kacey (divorced mom and stepmom): *"Over the past two years, my husband has surprised me with the patience and understanding to discuss the challenges we have dealt with regarding his high-conflict ex-wife. He looks at the situation, how his reaction might be taken and does his best to protect the children from any conflict between the two of them. I'm also thankful for the relationship my husband has with my children as they are older. He's the perfect stepfather!"*

T.D. (divorced mom, stepmom): *"I truly believed before that men did* not *fall in love. I didn't believe it, I* knew *it. I'm so, so happy to be proven wrong by my husband."*

Matty (stepmom): *"I think because this was my second go at it, I was less shocked at what happened. I felt like my husband respected me and included me as part of the family by talking to me about daily decisions. I think it also has helped us figure out how we complement each other's parenting styles and figure out how we want to parent our 'ours' kids. My stepson has always been kind and receptive overall, so that made it easier. His mom temporarily acted out, but my husband anticipated this and called her out every time. Their interactions have been up and down through everything. He became more assertive with his own boundaries though, and I think it was good for my stepson and for our family unit."*

CHECKLIST: HOW ARE YOU OVERLOOKING WHAT YOUR PARTNER OR EX IS GIVING?

Place a checkmark next to any of the behaviors you recognize in your ex or your husband below. Ways a man shows his love that you may not recognize:

- coaching an after-school activity or sport
- teaching the child manual skills, such as how to build or fix something
- leading by example: keeping his word, helping others
- being attentive, i.e., asks about your day or the kid's day
- following up on discussions he's had with you before, especially things you or the kids are worried about
- being affectionate
- encouraging and/or helping the children provide holiday gifts for his ex or his wife
- going to work every day to earn a living and providing for your home
- paying child support on time or early
- fixing mechanical things around the house
- sharing technological knowledge with the kids
- helping with homework
- roughhousing with the kids on the floor or mussing up their hair, tickling, etc.

JOURNAL QUESTIONS:
MY PARTNER'S OR EX'S CONTRIBUTIONS

What did you learn about the ways in which your husband or the children's father is actively expressing his love to you or the children? Have you been overlooking any of these contributions and discounting them?

_____

_____

_____

STEPPING UP OR SLACKING OFF

One of the main complaints we often hear from moms regarding their ex-husbands is that if he's remarried and the stepmom plays an active parenting role, then he is being "let off the hook." Dad doesn't have to step up to the plate. He can fade quietly into the background.

It may be painful for divorced moms to see that men who divorce can indeed change, grow, and actually be better parents and partners—with someone else. Many stepmoms agree that their husbands are 2.0 versions of their former selves and ultimately, that's a good thing for all parties involved.

There are three possible variations of what a father can become after divorce and remarriage:

1. He hasn't changed. He was disinterested and uninvolved before as a parent and partner and still is.
2. He has become a better partner, but still practices a more hands-off approach to parenting, compared to mom.
3. He has become a noticeably better partner *and* a better father.

It's easy to confuse numbers 2 and 3 above. This goes back to the differences between how men and women (especially mothers and fathers) show their love. But as we discussed earlier, women will often step up to the plate without even being asked. The stepmoms in the second group who fulfill some of the parenting duties for their husbands out of love and partnership might actually be enabling some pretty unhealthy behavior—for the children's sake — and for themselves.

We mentioned competing loyalties and instincts in Chapter 1. Research shows that for the marriage between a father and stepmother to survive, it must take priority over all other relationships. This can be confusing as you wonder, *Wait, how does that work? Doesn't that sound like neglecting the kids?* Absolutely not. As Mario stated earlier, the kids are his first responsibility, but his marriage is his first priority. The children's needs must continue to be met, but you must also negotiate some difficult questions. Who's going to handle the enforcement of rules in the household after a father remarries? Who determines consequences for breaking those rules? Each "side" involved can have very different ideas about how discipline should be handled.

In the instance of the third scenario above, these fathers have remarried and, as in any healthy marriage, their partners have become integrated into their lives. Stepmoms will often do almost anything to make the life of their husband and his kids better or easier (granted, many times to her detriment). But here's the part that we think moms are missing when they confuse a dad who's not doing his part with one who's truly involved—he and his second wife are doing what happy, functional couples do by practicing reciprocity. And if there are now two adults in this household to raise and love the children, instead of one, why is that seen as dad escaping his responsibilities? This phrase makes it sound like he weaseled his way out of his parenting duties. Absolutely, there are some dads who are guilty of this. But there are plenty of them who aren't.

More likely, good dads have made room to let their partners help with things that women are typically better at, such as appointments, scheduling and reminders about household tasks. Moms, would you not jump at the opportunity to have some help on your end? If you have remarried yourself and you have a helpful partner, then you know what it's like!

IN THE WORDS OF OUR READERS

Tamara M. (stepmom): *"When my husband started seeing himself as being in an equal partnership with me, everything changed. Initially, he viewed his leadership role as consisting of sacrificing for our family and protecting us. Eventually he took on more of a supportive role by listening to me, addressing my emotional needs and upholding my decisions, especially when a difficult circumstance presented itself. I think he realized that the children wouldn't feel neglected or suffer just because he made a strong commitment to the 'new spouse.' He didn't have to choose between me and the girls (my two stepdaughters) and started making our marriage his primary priority. He realized he was choosing both. Placing me first and having a healthy marriage means safety and protection for all of our children (my stepdaughters and my son)."*

K.B. (divorced mom, stepmom): *"My husband has greatly surprised me by being a very hands-on parent. I assumed that once we were married, I would do more 'mom' type things for the stepkids. Nope. He wants to do it. At first, I was hurt and felt shut out. Once I talked to him about it, he explained he didn't want me to feel he was dumping his parenting responsibilities on me."*

Michelle (stepmom): *"When my 12-year-old stepson would spend all afternoon gaming and wait until 9 pm to do his homework, it would drive me nuts. I just wasn't raised that way. I used to always look at my husband with a 'Are you really going to allow that?' look and it would inevitably cause friction between us. I finally started learning that it's not my place to tell him how to parent. It didn't do any good anyways, so I stopped. Then one day when my stepson was complaining that he was too tired to do his homework but had a big project due, I heard my husband say from the other room, 'That's what you get for waiting until the last minute. No more gaming before homework. From now on, it's homework first.' I was so proud of him. I don't think it ever would have happened if I kept harping on him, making him feel bad about himself as a parent."*

QUIZ—MAKING HIM WRONG (FOR DIVORCED MOMS ONLY)

Place a checkmark next to every sentence that you identify with over the other. Which statements can you relate to? Is it possible that the second statement in each group is more true than you'd like to admit?

> *He should do everything himself as a dad or he's lazy.*
> Versus
> *It helps everyone if he has an involved partner, especially the kids.*

> *If I don't get any help from a partner, then he shouldn't, either.*
> Versus
> *We all need help in life. I wish I could have my own wife!*

> *He's hurting the kids and he doesn't care.*
> Versus
> *He really does love them and they know it. But he has his own way and it's just as good as mine.*

If he doesn't show the kids that he loves them like I do, he's damaging them irreparably.

Versus

I have to admit, I know they feel secure in the knowledge that their dad would do anything for them.

JOURNAL QUESTIONS

Moms, what do you think about what you checked off above? Are you making assumptions about how your ex is slacking off, when he really just has his own style? What can you appreciate about him as a father? How is he giving more to the kids than you realized?

_____

_____

_____

QUIZ—MAKING HIM WRONG (FOR STEPMOMS ONLY)

Place a checkmark next to every sentence that you prefer over the other. Which statements can you relate to? Is it possible that the second statement in each group is more true than you'd like to admit?

He's missing yet another *opportunity to teach the children a life lesson about responsibility!*

Versus

He knows what he's doing and not everything has to be a lesson learned.

He's spoiling his kids by doing for them what they can be doing for themselves.

Versus

He's showing love for his kids by providing for them.

He should never do anything nice for his ex-wife.

Versus

He's a provider by nature and by being nice to her he keeps conflict away from his family.

He doesn't care about me or anyone else. He's shut down and won't talk to me about what's going on.
Versus
He's processing what happened and needs to be left alone to do that. He will talk to me when he's ready.

JOURNAL QUESTIONS

Stepmoms, what do you think about what you checked off above? Are there any areas where you're overlooking your husband's contributions? What aren't you giving him credit for? Are there any areas where you can show him that you trust him to do the right thing by taking a step back?

_____

_____

_____

IN THE WORDS OF OUR READERS

L. B. (stepmom): *"When my husband and I started dating, I was very involved, some might say overly involved. It didn't bother the mom of my oldest stepdaughter (at least that I know of), but it did bother the mom of my youngest stepdaughter. She was very vocal about it. Over the years, she relaxed some and understood that my husband involved me, not because he didn't want to deal with things, but because I was a part of his family. When things were fine between us all, she never mentioned my involvement. She actually would involve me, herself. But when things took a turn for the worse, I was enemy number one and she didn't want to 'deal' with me at all. Things got pretty ugly for a while there. I also think a lot of the times my husband would use the word 'we' (meaning himself and me) whenever he would talk to his ex. She would automatically hear my 'voice' in this instead of his and she would* *get defensive. I think it drove her to resent me. I let him know that it probably would be best if he refrained from involving me in their conversations. She didn't need that in her face. Things are better now that he practices that with her and their correspondence seems to be less emotional and more 'business-like now.'"*

J.W. (stepmom): *"I think I went into my relationship very worried. I had never been with a man who had children. I feared I would always come second and that I would always feel insecure. But my husband manages to be an amazing dad to all of his kids (now to include 'ours') and to always prioritize our relationship and our marriage. He has completely allayed all of my fears."*

COMMUNICATION AND EMASCULATION

Although men can be big and burly, many are actually quite sensitive to what they perceive as criticism, which doesn't inspire them to change, but to turn off instead. For example, you might want to discuss a concern about his kids or a parenting decision he's made, and before you can finish your thought, he's either defensive and/or has found his way into the garage.

Stepmoms, hopefully your husband has read Mario's chapter and will take his advice about listening to you when you have a concern. But if not, a good rule of thumb when it comes to men is: don't give unsolicited advice. Because when you do, he's likely to *think* one or all of the following:

- you're criticizing him as a man
- you don't trust him to handle the problem competently
- you think he's a bad parent

And he's likely to *respond* in one or all of the following ways:

- shut down and not want to discuss it—ever
- get defensive and not be able to hear anything you're saying
- feel so beaten down that he loses faith in his ability to meet your needs

When we said that men are sensitive to criticism, we weren't joking. If your tone even *slightly* resembles that of a mother scolding her child, you may lose his attention and piss him off. If you roll your eyes or question him, you may have just blown your chance at sparking his natural desire to make you happy. This goes for stepmoms *and* divorced moms. Criticism and unsolicited advice are two of the main ways in which women unknowingly emasculate men, and are the quickest ways to ensure he'll feel resentful toward you and have no interest in hearing what you have to say.

It comes down to trust. Men *need* to know you trust them. This alone can alter a relationship dynamic that's been toxic for years. The belief that you're on his side and feel confident his attempts will succeed is what allows him to trust *you*. Telling him that while criticizing him isn't going to cut it. He needs to see proof. He needs to see the data.

So where to begin? Start by letting him know how much you appreciate him on a regular basis and by changing the way you interact with him. For divorced moms, this may mean not communicating so often and respecting his new relationship. For divorced moms *and* stepmoms, this may mean not voicing your opinion about his parenting shortcomings, as you see them. As long as the kids aren't being abused, let him parent how he sees fit. Expect and *accept* that it won't be how *you* would parent and may not be up to your standards. Keep reminding yourself that he's *fathering*, not mothering. He'll be able to learn and grow if he feels supported. He can't and won't if he feels you're against him. For tips on how to express appreciation, see the "How to Talk to a Man" section below.

"PROCESSING" EMOTIONS

Women can't stand silence if they think that someone is potentially upset with them. We feel compelled to poke at men's emotions and have them tell us everything they're thinking so we can be reassured we are still loved and wanted. The problem with this is that most men process their emotions by working on projects, completing tasks, fixing something, playing video games—basically by doing anything they can do *alone*. Doesn't that just drive us crazy? We feel better by *talking* and they feel better by *not*. So if you're persistently trying to pull words out of him while he's mulling over an issue, you'll find him becoming more distant. Focus on another way to get your needs met and give him his space. He'll come back to you sooner, feeling more grounded and able to readily share what was going on with him.

IN THE WORDS OF OUR READERS

> **K.K. (divorced mom, stepmom):** *"My second husband surprised me with his absolute refusal to blame me for my children's bad behaviour. My ex always made their behaviour my fault. If I was there, then 'I hadn't supervised properly.' If I wasn't and he was, it was because 'I hadn't taught them properly.' At the beginning of my current marriage, every time the girls misbehaved I was so worried he would get angry with me and begin to hate me. I can't tell you my relief to know that he sees my children's behaviour as entirely separate from me. I think our refusal to blame each other for our kids is one of the biggest things that makes our relationship work so well."*

> **Matty (stepmom):** *"My husband seems like the emotionally clueless nerd, kind of like Sheldon. But if I need to talk or something is up, he is a great listener and tries to get it. It does surprise me when he gets short with my stepson and it tends to be when his ex-wife has irritated him. But now that I've pointed out this trend, he is more conscious of it and is trying to get rid of it."*

HOW-TO: COMMUNICATING WITH A MAN

EXPRESSING APPRECIATION

If you're having trouble coming up with how to support or show appreciation to your husband or ex-husband (especially if don't particularly like him or feel wronged by him), try thinking of something nice he did for the kids recently, no matter how small. Does he work and help to support them financially? Did he help with a school project or teach them something recently? Did he pick the kids up on time or take an extra parenting day? Express your gratitude. It doesn't take much to change your relationship. Even ones with long-standing hurt or resentment can be quickly improved by the expression of gratitude for things we normally take for granted.

Here are some sample phrases to try:

- "You're such a great husband and father, thank you for ____"
- "Thank you so much for cleaning up the kitchen tonight, you really provided me with a stress-free evening!"
- "Even though we have our differences, you're a good father and I'm thankful for that."
- "Thanks so much for taking the kids even though it wasn't your weekend. I really appreciated it."

TROUBLESHOOTING PROBLEMS

Be curious instead of making assumptions or accusations. Ask his thoughts on the matter. Invite him to help you come up with a solution to your issue. Remember, men love to fix problems. If you have a contentious relationship with your ex, enrolling him in brainstorming a problem conveys respect for his opinions, and you never know, it may make getting along easier *for* both of you. Be sure to make your request, clear, succinct and actionable and if you like, include some simple information about how solving this problem will help either you or others.

Some sample questions:

- "When would be a good time to talk? I just need about 10 minutes." (Hint: not when he's at work or in his man cave.)
- "How do you think we can resolve this issue of ___ (insert problem here)? What are some of your ideas on this?"
- "I've been feeling ___, and what would really help me is if you could ____."
- "You know, if we could make it so that _____ (desired change), it would really help me feel much more relaxed in the evenings, so we could spend some time together (or other statement about the benefits of having this problem handled)."

Communicating with him differently will help him know that you *trust* him (maybe only in particular areas, but nevertheless, focus on what's possible here, instead of what's not). In difficult relationships with consistent animosity (perhaps especially those), helping the other person feel respected in at least a few *specific* areas can be transformative.

JOURNAL QUESTIONS: HOW I COMMUNICATE WITH MEN

How can you communicate differently with your partner or your ex? In what ways have you unknowingly been emasculating him? What ideas do you have for communicating with him differently from now on?

_____

_____

COMING INTO THEIR OWN AS DADS

Men don't need us to micromanage their relationships as fathers. Just because they're not parenting as we women would prefer, doesn't mean they're doing a poor job. But many women are uncomfortable leaving any kind of *vacuum* for a father to step into. We see them hesitate and we step on their toes without giving them a chance to figure it out or learn something new.

It doesn't matter if you're a divorced mom or a stepmom. By keeping your truly nonessential judgments about his parenting to yourself, you give him space to learn and grow as a father. Some men just did what their first wives wanted them to do because it was easier than being criticized. Now that they're no longer married to their first wife, they've discovered that they can be the parent *they* want to be with their own choices and style. There may be some stumbling along the path as with anything that you learn for the first time, but eventually they'll find their way. Give them the chance to blossom as a father. Their children's lives will be all the richer for it.

IN THE WORDS OF OUR READERS

> **Chelle (stepmom):** *"After vowing to 'never date a guy with children,' I ran into an old friend, eventually met his children and*

instantly fell in love with the father he is. Growing up, he didn't have good examples of what a father should be, but he follows his heart and is one of the most incredible dads I've ever known. He is involved, caring, patient, and protective of his boys. Watching the 'kid' I knew in middle school raise two amazing young men and then having him allow me to help raise them alongside him is an incredibly powerful thing. He has blown my mind over and over with the parent he's become."

J.B. (divorced mom): *"I was really nervous when I was pregnant with our 'ours' baby because my husband was never really a man who thought he wanted kids. He was loving toward my boys, but I felt some hesitation there. I knew it came from the conflict from my ex-husband, but part of me wondered if he regretted the family-man lifestyle he was a part of once he married me. Now our baby is 19 months old and he has been in my boys' lives for almost 4 years. He is a great dad and that has made him an even better stepdad, way more well rounded. I think seeing parenting from the beginning gave him more perspective and made him realize that structure and discipline are important, but so are all the millions of things big and small that make up parenthood."*

JOURNAL QUESTIONS: SUPPORTING MEN AS FATHERS

Moms, are you possibly setting your ex up to fail because you're still hurt and angry with him? How can you show respect and support for his path as a father? How might this help the kids?

_____

_____

Stepmoms, how can you let go of what *you* think is best for his kids and let him be the father he is? How can you better support his decisions, even if you don't fully agree with them?

_____

_____

CHECK YOUR THINKING

POTENTIAL NEGATIVE BELIEFS

Here are some examples of negative beliefs you might not realize you have. Put a checkmark next to any you can relate to:

- I just can't trust men.
- I always have to pry a man's true feelings out of him.
- Men always hurt and betray me.
- Men are impossible to figure out.
- Men don't care about anyone but themselves.
- Men are clueless about what women and children need.
- Men are inherently lazy.
- Men don't know how to show love.
- I can never be myself with a man.

What are your thoughts about what you checked off?

_____

_____

_____

INCREASING YOUR POSITIVE BELIEFS

It's possible to dramatically improve the quality of your life by deliberately increasing the number of affirming beliefs "automatically" available to your conscious and unconscious mind. Use the following mantras or affirmations on a daily basis, inputting them into your subconscious twice a day or during a focused meditation. Your choice!

ACCESSING YOUR SUBCONSCIOUS—TWICE A DAY

Contrary to outdated opinion, we actually *can* reshape long-standing, subconscious beliefs. Repeat the affirmations (listed below) to yourself during times of extra stress or, for best results, for a week or two upon rising or falling asleep. During those two times in particular, you are in a theta brain state and your subconscious mind is at its most impressionable.

MEDITATION: FEELING GOOD IN YOUR OWN SKIN

Follow the steps listed for Meditation in Section Two, Power Tools, to guide yourself into a nice, relaxed state, then silently repeat any of the following mantras. Take as much time as you need and let any other thoughts float by and fade away. If you find yourself drifting off into a state of "argument" with an affirmation, gently refocus your attention, return to the statement and enhance any feelings of softness, warmth and expansion in your heart. Continue until you feel better...

POTENTIAL POSITIVE BELIEFS

Choose two or three that resonate with you and mentally repeat each one, as you breathe slowly and deeply.

- Men are happy to protect me and our family.
- Men are loving and kind.
- I can trust the men in my life to treat me with love.
- Men are wonderful, mysterious creatures.
- I allow the men in my life to have complementary skills.
- It's easy to work together with men.
- I create peaceful, happy relationships with men.
- I forgive the men in my life for past hurts.
- The children benefit from their father's unique love and knowledge.
- I am safe with men.
- I can allow men to grow and change at their own pace.
- I learn how to be a better parent by learning from their dad.
- I love men.

CHAPTER 11

EXPECTATIONS: MAKING PROGRESS
(self-control vs. controlling her)

IMPOSSIBLY HIGH STANDARDS

Let's talk for a moment about the Catch-22 of having expectations that no one on earth could ever possibly meet: those you might have for the other woman and the other household. When it comes to how you expect the other woman to behave, could you meet the same standards you've set for her? Think about it:

- Never say a bad word about her.
- Always do what's best for the children (according to your private interpretation).
- Never be late (come hell, high water or bad traffic).
- Never get angry, be snippy, play the victim, or be a flake.

Life is messy. You solve five problems and ten others line up to take their place. We all know it—everyone drops the ball on a daily basis. Doesn't life just seem impossible in some ways? We talked about support in Chapter Two and how it helps to vent about our problems. To our friends, co-workers, even perfect strangers (and yes, even with the kids or stepkids, though we know we're not supposed to). We seek comfort and reassurance. We connect and gain support.

If we're doing it right, we use venting *temporarily* to release pressure just like a pressure cooker's bobbing weight lets off extra steam. We release stress and tension with sympathetic friends so that we can then *take action*. We take action to hopefully *fix the problem* (while nine others unravel in the background).

We're *trying!*

But think about it. If you regularly nail the other woman (or someone else in their household) because she has the audacity to vent and present a skewed analysis of the situation, you will always be unhappy. She likely thinks you're doing the same thing.

If you condemn her because she dared express a negative emotion such as anger, frustration, self-righteousness, competitiveness, or self-pity while refusing to consider that she might also be trying to find a temporary, *empowering* response to a difficult situation (just like you), then your own emotional reactions to her will remain in a constant state of agitation.

If you automatically assume her behavior is deliberate when it comes to mistakes you would easily excuse in yourself because of the natural chaos of being human, you will continue to feel under siege as if she's doing these things *on purpose* to make your life miserable. You can't apply one standard to yourself and a completely separate one to her. She is, after all, *just a person.* Like you.

JOURNAL QUESTIONS:
MY STANDARDS FOR HER AND OTHERS

In what areas is she expected to never drop the ball?

_____

_____

In what ways do you "excuse" yourself from having to modify your own unhelpful behavior?

_____

_____

What might happen if you held her to the standards you normally apply to *yourself* and those you love?

_____

_____

"Incredible change happens in your life when you decide to take control of what you do have power over, instead of craving control over what you don't."
– Steve Maraboli

DECIDE TO STOP CONTROLLING HER

Don't you find clichés galling? How many times have we all heard "The only person you can control is yourself"? Sure, you know *intellectually* that you can't change someone else's behavior to fit your needs, yet you may continue to *insist* somehow in your head:

> *"Maybe if I'm nicer to her..."*
> *"Maybe if I appease her..."*
> *"Maybe if I ignore her..."*
> *"Maybe if I kill her with kindness..."*
> *"Maybe if I just model how a* real *grown-up would do it..."*
> "Then, she will ___."

These are all *still* attempts to manipulate her behavior.

People in high-emotional conflict cannot see your good intentions or hear words meant to help. In *some* cases we can give others a new perspective that might lead to insight on their behalf, but this usually only happens with people we already have an established relationship with. Not quite the description of your relationship with the mom or stepmom in your life, right?

As we talked about in Chapter Four on expectations, there's also the influence of different *values*. If you completed the Values exercise in Section One, you might have determined that you each have a very different set of values. You're not going to change hers, just like she can't convince you that yours are wrong. Can you leave space open for both sets of values? Can you both be right? How would it benefit the kids to have a wider view on life? Remember how easy it is for our values to clash and conflict, instead of jumping to the conclusion that her decisions are based on character flaws.

On the other hand, none of us are saints. We know it's lousy to feel like *you're* the only one sucking it up and shouldering all the weight, but if you want to create positive change, you must conciously accept responsibility. That means, right now, right here in this moment while you're reading this book, you must say to yourself (silently or out loud):

*I'm going to stop trying to change and control her.
I'm going to focus instead on where I can actually make a difference—and that's
with myself. From this point on, I will stop the behavior that is not getting me
anywhere.*

Are you constantly pushing yourself to be "the better person," but still competing with the other woman to come out on top? Whatever is going on with
her, whatever is fueling her unwanted behavior, realize that the cause is bigger
than you. Release yourself from this burden of trying to make her change.
Lighten your load. Honor your own moral standards as best you can and repeat
to yourself, *"I am not responsible for her actions. I release the need to control her."*
Since most of us have been pressuring ourselves to change for years, it's a bit
unrealistic to think you can just snap your fingers and you'll be cured of manipulating yourself or anyone else. So be prepared: there will be times when a part
of you still wants to hold her responsible and *force* her to do things differently
so you can be more comfortable and happy. When you can, catch yourself in the
act, course correct and prevent the downward mental spiral that usually follows.
Focus on what *is* your responsibility, the dynamic in your household, and
make changes as you see fit. See how you can create less worrying. More laughing. Less stress. More fun. Less anger. More love.

Jennifer R. (stepmom): *"I had a relationship with my stepchild's
mom that was beyond crazy at first. When we ignored her and
didn't give her access to us, it made things worse. One day, I called
her and we said everything we needed to say. I even apologized to
her if I'd ever hurt her in any way. From there, the healing began
and we started to parent together and bounce ideas off each other.
It was in the best interest of the child to get along and now, we
actually live in peace. When you have two separate parenting styles
and completely different rules for the children, it confuses the child
about how to behave. If a child knows he can get away with a
certain behavior at one house, it causes a problem with the other
house. Now we have an open line of communication with mom
and it helps to keep the child's behavior in check. A lot of drama
is created when the parties are not a united front. Despite your*

dislike for the other parent, getting along as a family is what the child really wants. Too many people get hung up on telling the other parent not to tell them what to do in their homes, but they are missing the big picture. You do not have to tell the other household every detail of your life or how you parent your child. However, when you communicate with the other parent about what works for you, or that the child got in trouble and I did this to correct his behavior, then the other parent is aware of the issue and that reinforces your authority with the child."

Lauren T. (stepmom): *"When there is lack of respect, everything else crumbles. There is name-calling, verbal attacks and tons of judgment. It creates two sides, rather than a team for the children. It affects school, homework and public events. It makes extra-curriculars impossible, due to lack of mutual support and communication. It takes the smallest issues and turns them into monumental ordeals. All of this ultimately hurts the child, because they see that the adults can't get along and it creates loyalty issues. Kids should be stopping to jump in mud puddles and investigating their curiosities—not in the middle of a war zone, watching shots being fired; picking sides, feeling guilty and embarrassed during their moments to shine. When there is respect, mistakes (which everyone makes!) can become learning experiences, rather than opportunities to blame and point fingers."*

CHANGING THE THINGS THAT DON'T WORK

If you're continually feeling dissatisfied with your situation, we suggest that there is a particular vision you're holding onto and resisting how things actually are. Think of someone who came to terms with a serious trauma, such as a terminal illness, losing a loved one, or getting fired from their job. Did you ever see this happen? As soon as they let go of their image of *how the experience should be*, they were able to find peace in the face of extreme challenges.

Review your answers in Chapter Four so we can do a little detective work with your expectations. A good question to unearth this information is to ask yourself "What is the ideal version of how I'd like things to be between the households?" For example:

> *Moms:* Do you wish the stepmom would just step back and let you and your ex handle all communications? Or would you rather talk to her than your difficult ex?
>
> *Stepmoms:* Do you wish mom would be friendly, make eye contact, or acknowledge your role in your stepchildren's life? Or do you wish she'd just stop contacting you?

You must get clear on what you want things to look like in your divorce-connected family. If you don't, your reactions and your behavior are going to be fueled by a murky agenda that will feel like a hidden force operating in the background, working against you (*even though it's you!*).

THREE SMALL CHANGES—THE OLD WAY

Now that you have a better awareness of how your "reasonable" beliefs create pressure for things to be a particular way, followed by conflict and eventual disappointment, you're ready to tackle making a few changes. The way to make big changes is to start small, so we want you to list three small changes you'd like to make in your life right now. To help you brainstorm, we've listed some questions to answer below.

What's currently not working?
What would you like to improve or modify?
What would make your life a lot easier?

Just as with our requests for support from men, think in terms of concrete, measurable changes. Would you be able to easily check these off on a chart if they were complete or not? Come up with small, simple actions, not big sweeping changes that set you up for failure.

Change #1

_____

_____

_____

Change #2

_____

_____

_____

Change #3

_____

_____

_____

Do any of these desired outcomes require *someone else* to do the changing? Notice if any of them begin with "I want *her* to…" or "*He* should…." Now we're going to reframe those changes in terms of you instead.

THREE SMALL CHANGES—WITH ONLY YOU

Look back at what you wrote above when describing what you wish your situation looked like. What are three small changes *within your control* that you can shoot for? Since you can truly only alter your behavior, what is within *your* power to change? If you need to start again and write down easier changes to shoot for, go ahead and do that now.

Ready? Good.

Pick *only one change to work on*, then read through (but don't answer yet) the following questions:

1. **What is one change you'd like to make?**
2. **List the obstacles you might face.** If you're having trouble anticipating possible hurdles, ask yourself these questions:

     a. What makes it hard to get this done?

     b. What external factors will have to be in place for this to work?

     c. What do you need now that you don't have?

     d. What do you gain from *not* making this change? What would you lose that's important to you if you made this change?

3. **What are some of the positive aspects this change would bring to your life?** What do you gain from making this change?

4. **What type of support system do you need to help you achieve these changes?** Think back to what you learned in Chapter Two about sabotaging, in-the-moment support versus truth-telling, healthy support.

Let's walk through an example together and then it will be your turn.

1. CHANGE I WANT TO MAKE:

When I receive an insulting and unwanted communication from the other woman, I'll wait at least one hour before responding.

Notice this is one *small* change. A bigger goal, or one in which this small goal might serve as a stepping stone could be, "When I receive an insulting and unwanted communication from the other woman, I will not respond and I will not obsess about it. I will remain calm and take it with a grain of salt."

2. POSSIBLE OBSTACLES:

Breaking my pattern of obsessing. I usually read an offending communication at least five times, then immediately draft a response in order to defend myself. Then I spend the next few hours upset at what was said about me and I'll call a friend to bitch to. Another possible obstacle is that my friends are all too happy to bash her. They enjoy hearing the gory details and encourage me to defend myself to her.

3. WHAT DO I GAIN FROM MAKING THIS CHANGE?

I'll get time and energy back if I'm not wasting it on defending myself and trying to change someone's mind about me or prove her wrong. I'll be in a more peaceful state of mind if I'm not perpetuating the drama by engaging her. I'll feel empowered knowing I don't need her approval or for her to like me in order to be happy and feel good about myself. I'll be in a better mood at work and around my family, since I won't spend hours stewing over what's going wrong, keeping a bad experience alive long after it's over.

4. WHAT TYPE OF SUPPORT SYSTEM DO I NEED TO HELP YOU ACHIEVE THESE CHANGES?

Friends and family to understand and support my goal, who won't sabotage me by gossiping or encouraging me to engage with her. People who understand dual-family dynamics and how difficult and challenging they can be. Friends who understand I may be tempted to slip back into subtle attempts to control or change her and what that behavior looks like in me, even if I can't see it at the time.

EXERCISE—ONE SMALL CHANGE TO MAKE

Your turn! What's one change that you'd like to focus on? What do you choose to improve in your life without waiting for anyone else to change?

_____

_____

List the obstacles you might face.

_____

_____

What are some of the positive aspects this change would bring to your life?
What do you gain from making this change?

_____

_____

What type of support system do you need to help you achieve these changes?
Think back to what you learned in Chapter Two about sabotaging, in-the-moment support and truth telling, healthy support.

_____

_____

JOURNAL QUESTIONS:
A NEW APPROACH TO MAKING CHANGES

What jumped out at you the most when you completed this exercise? How do you feel now about attempting these changes by focusing only on your own behavior instead of hers? Can you brainstorm any additional ways to overcome the obstacles you described above? What kind of support will you line up for yourself to stay on track?

_____

_____

While you may be wishing you could fix all the problems between you and the other woman, the primary goal here is to tweak the circumstances of your life so that you're increasing your _own_ feelings of competence and self-control, and shrugging off the things that don't matter.

A WORD ABOUT THE SERIOUSLY
CHALLENGING OTHER WOMAN

If you're thinking this chapter doesn't apply to you because your counterpart is on the far end of the bad-behavior continuum (i.e. has attempted to get you fired from your job, lied in court, etc.), there's still hope for you. After all, this book isn't meant to bring you two together as best friends; it's to teach you how to find peace, regardless of how off her rocker she may or may not be (in your opinion). It's still apropos to notice what your expectations are and align them with the *actual* situation.

In Chapter Thirteen, we'll show you how to be firm and consistent with new boundaries. If you feel the need to jump ahead to limit setting, revisit Chapter Six for an in-depth discussion on the problems with inconsistent boundaries and read Chapter Thirteen for helpful tools.

For the high-conflict counterpart, we refer you to resources that specialize in managing these types of relationships. One such book is *It's All Your Fault: 12 Tips for Managing People Who Blame Others for Everything*, written by Bill Eddy, LCSW. This book explains how the behaviors of high-conflict people are largely unconscious and how any attempt to prove they're wrong may only serve to increase their aggressive reactions toward you and perpetuate conflict. It can take more than just healthy boundaries to protect yourself from the behavior of high-conflict people, so we urge you to seek out support and information that's specific to this personality type.

It can be so freeing to realize that regardless of what she says or thinks about you, it ultimately doesn't matter. Her behavior says more about *her* than it does about you. It's not personal, though it may feel like it. You aren't the final interpreter of what her behavior actually means anyway, right? You only know what *you* think about it.

Now that the focus is on you, are you starting to realize that you have always had more power than you knew to improve your situation? It's true!

CHECK YOUR THINKING

POTENTIAL NEGATIVE BELIEFS

Here are some examples of negative beliefs you might not realize you have. Put a checkmark next to any you can relate to:

- I must anticipate everyone's next move so I can control the situation.
- My needs are more important than hers.
- I'm the only one who can see how things should *really* be done.
- I always have to be in control or someone will screw me over.

- She will always react poorly to me, no matter what.
- I must change how she feels about me.
- If I'm not one step ahead of her, she'll ruin everything for me.
- If I give in to her demands, she'll see that I'm a good, nice person.
- If we all don't get along, people will think something is wrong with me.
- I have to prove that she can't affect me.
- If you want something done right, you have to do it yourself.

What are your thoughts about what you checked off?

_____

_____

_____

INCREASING YOUR POSITIVE BELIEFS

It's possible to dramatically improve the quality of your life by deliberately increasing the number of affirming beliefs "automatically" available to your conscious and unconscious mind. Use the following mantras or affirmations on a daily basis, inputting them into your subconscious twice a day or during a focused meditation. Your choice!

ACCESSING YOUR SUBCONSCIOUS—TWICE A DAY

Contrary to outdated opinion, we actually _can_ reshape long-standing, subconscious beliefs. Repeat the affirmations (listed below) to yourself during times of extra stress or, for best results, for a week or two upon rising or falling asleep. During those two times in particular, you are in a theta brain state and your subconscious mind is at its most impressionable.

MEDITATION: FEELING GOOD IN YOUR OWN SKIN

Follow the steps listed for Meditation in Section Two, Power Tools, to guide yourself into a nice, relaxed state, then silently repeat any of the following mantras. Take as much time as you need and let any other thoughts float by and fade away. If you find yourself drifting off into a state of "argument" with an affirmation, gently refocus your attention, return to the statement and enhance any feelings of softness, warmth and expansion in your heart. Continue until you feel better.

POTENTIAL POSITIVE BELIEFS

Choose two or three that resonate with you and mentally repeat each one, as you breathe slowly and deeply.

- There is a higher purpose.
- We all have our own truth.
- I trust others to do their part.
- We're all in this together.
- It's safe to release control.
- The important things are covered.
- I easily accept the contributions of others.
- Everyone's needs are equally important.
- It's okay to not have a relationship with her.
- I'm a good and loving person.
- I accept my responsibilities and leave others to theirs.
- I am flexible and resilient.
- I trust others to do what they need to do.
- I focus on what is within my control.

CHAPTER 12

SELF-WORTH: MAKING PROGRESS

(letting her determine your self-esteem vs. generating your own)

FEELING BETTER ABOUT YOU

In the following section, we present a variety of tools to help you start feeling better about yourself. Some of these can be done while you're sitting at your desk at work or driving in the car. Others can be done in a private space when you have some extra time to dedicate to the task. Each tool works in a different way, so we recommend going through them at least once, then sticking with what resonates with you.

We know that taking a deep look at yourself can be scary. But you and your family deserve access to the best you possible.

STEP-BY-STEP: HOW TO LOVE YOURSELF RIGHT NOW

You actually *can* begin healing yourself right now without going through years and years of therapy or requiring someone else to rescue you by loving and accepting you *first*. The following technique is deceptively simple and can be done in less than a minute. It might feel a bit abstract at first, but give it a try, because once you *feel* your way through this, *you'll really get it*. It's a solid tool to lean on during difficult times. Staying rooted inside yourself during the blustery winds of life makes all of your problems seem more manageable. The exercise below is a unique blend of steps from two books: John Welwood's *Perfect Love, Imperfect Relationships* and *The HeartMath Solution* by Doc Lew Childre, Howard Martin and Donna Beech.

Welwood's principal theory is that most of our emotional pain comes from shutting our hearts down to protect ourselves (ironic, huh?). Unfortunately, those attempts to shield ourselves from upset only lead to further agony because the natural state of our hearts is to *be open*. Basically, everything gets caught in the net of constriction of a closed heart. *The closing off is what actually hurts.*

HeartMath adheres to similar principles, but is a research-based approach to helping people harness the "intelligence and guidance of their own hearts" using emotional physiology, neurocardiology, resilience and cutting-edge, stress management discoveries. People have been saying, "Follow your heart," for thousands of years across cultures. That's because the heart really *does* have its own native wisdom, with stores of serotonin that rival those of the brain. According to HeartMath, we can use our hearts to rinse away and dissolve painful emotions, almost like a dishwasher with its own built-in garbage disposal.

To create more self-love, follow these three steps below. (A more in-depth exercise follows that you can apply to tougher problems. But let's start with feeling better about yourself first.)

The three basic steps are:
1. Stop resisting and rejecting yourself because of your problems.
2. Focus on something or someone that makes you happy for ten seconds.
3. Increase the feeling of joy and appreciation until it fills your whole body, let it shift to love, then direct it at yourself.

Let's look at each step one at a time.

1. STOP RESISTING AND REJECTING YOURSELF BECAUSE OF YOUR PROBLEMS

This first step might be one of the hardest because when we don't feel good, we just want to reject *everything*: our emotions, other people's feelings and actions, the immediate future and especially *ourselves*. We may be frustrated and overwhelmed by the intensity of our emotions, even if they are of the "softer" variety, such as sadness or hurt. We'd give practically anything not to be where we are right now: stuck with ourselves and our current experience.

The antidote to this is radical self-acceptance, even if you don't like or respect yourself in that moment. You make a conscious decision:

Resolve to accept all of you, just as you are right now, without changing anything.

Agree to be on your side as a reliable, consistent ally, with your gloriously flawed self. Say to yourself "I accept myself exactly as I am, right now." Then take a deep breath. Or several. Remember to make the out-breath longer than the in-breath, so it doesn't feel forced.

2. FOCUS ON SOMETHING OR SOMEONE THAT MAKES YOU HAPPY FOR TEN SECONDS

According to HeartMath principles, focusing on someone (or something) that you know automatically makes you happy brings your entire system into "coherence," with your nervous system and your heart working together. Your cortisol (a stress hormone) levels decrease, your immune system antibodies go up, and your anxiety levels start to drop.

Think about something that gives you a guaranteed good feeling without any "background" conflicts, like the softness and warmth of a beloved pet or the melting joy of hugging a child you love. Perhaps the memory of physical exercise always makes you smile, like thinking of taking a walk with the sun shining on your face while feeling strong and free.

Keep thinking these thoughts and focus on this feeling for at least ten seconds. Imagine yourself breathing in and out through your heart. Then go to the next step.

3. INCREASE THE FEELING OF JOY AND APPRECIATION UNTIL IT FILLS YOUR WHOLE BODY, LET IT SHIFT TO LOVE, THEN DIRECT IT AT YOURSELF

Stay with the feelings of joy and appreciation, then see if you can brighten them and widen them. Allow them to fill your entire body, reaching into even the tiniest spaces, like the tips of your fingers, toes and ears. Imagine them radiating out from your heart like a bright, shining sun and envision the sunlight streaming into your body, from the inside out. Sense the warmth and brilliance of your appreciation and joy and let it turn into a familiar feeling of love, if it hasn't already.

Remember what it feels like to be in love with another person? This may feel very similar, but now you're going to direct this powerful feeling of love toward yourself. Allow the love to completely fill you up. Relax in it. Soak in it. Breathe it in. There's nothing for you to do but simply love yourself.

Anytime you need a dose of love and compassion, give it to yourself!

USING YOUR HEART TO DISSOLVE DIFFICULT EMOTIONS

You can also use your heart to help you lessen difficult emotions that are persistently troubling you. The beauty here is that you're not "thinking your way through" or analyzing your problems with this technique. You're using a combination of breath work and the awesome power of your heart to create progress and keep your heart open and loving, for yourself and others.

You'll use the first three steps from above with a few more added on. To use your heart to dissolve difficult emotions:

1. Stop resisting and rejecting yourself because of your problems.
2. Focus on something or someone that makes you happy for ten seconds.
3. Increase the feeling of joy and appreciation until it fills your whole body, let it shift to love, then direct it at yourself.
4. Feel compassion for yourself and your suffering.
5. "Soak" your difficult feelings in your heart, just like soaking dirty dishes.
6. Ask your heart for any guidance or wisdom it has to share.

4. FEEL COMPASSION FOR YOURSELF AND YOUR SUFFERING

Are you a kind and nurturing friend? Do you treat the people you love with tenderness and warmth when they're feeling down? Do you judge them when they are hurting, feeling lost and overwhelmed? Likely not. Now it's time to conjure up that same generosity and apply a little kindness and tenderness to yourself. Go through steps one through three, as outlined above. Once you are "sitting" in love for yourself, rest your attention in your heart and see if you find any feelings of gentleness and compassion for yourself. Be patient about sensing this while taking deep, easy breaths. You deserve to be held and comforted when you're upset too. Choose to do this for yourself in this moment.

5. "SOAK" YOUR DIFFICULT FEELINGS IN YOUR HEART, JUST LIKE SOAKING DIRTY DISHES

Now for the fun part. There's nothing you have to "make" happen here. You're not looking for a mind-blowing insight, but if it happens, great. In this step, imagine taking the big ball of upset you're experiencing right now and placing it in your heart, this vast, powerful, ever-reliable machine at the center of your body. Trust in the ability of your heart to break down the *density* and intensity of your negative feelings while continuing to take slow, deep breaths. Visualize your heart "holding" and containing your upset and creating lightness, dissolving it into smaller and smaller pieces until it's barely discernible. Let your heart create ease and peace within you. Let your heart work its healing magic. If you have time, continue on until you feel a tangible shift. If not, just know you're still taking important steps to reduce your inner chaos and bring yourself back to balance.

6. ASK YOUR HEART FOR ANY GUIDANCE OR WISDOM IT HAS TO SHARE

Go ahead and ask your heart directly, "Do you have any wisdom or guidance for me now?" and see what pops up. You may hear a single word or a phrase. You might not hear anything at all and have something come to mind later. Whatever the result, don't push for some miraculous cure to your concerns at the moment. Just trust that you've made valuable progress in working together with your heart to tend to troubled emotions and give thanks for any feelings of increased equilibrium.

JOURNAL QUESTIONS:
WHAT MY HEART HAD TO SAY

What did you discover during this exercise? What simple lessons or insights would you like to remind yourself of later during times of stress and upset?

_____

_____

The goal isn't to completely eliminate any false beliefs you may repeatedly stumble upon, because that's nearly impossible. It's to make them occur less frequently by bringing them to the surface of your consciousness, acknowledging them, and then reminding yourself that they aren't true. It gets easier to do this over time. You'll get faster at it. Your heart is a wise guide that's always ready to help, if you let it.

FORGIVENESS

> *"To forgive is to set a prisoner free and discover that the prisoner was you." – Lewis B. Smedes*

It's easy to cross the line into anger and upset with someone else and then turn it upon ourselves, without realizing it. Whether we are nursing wounds, stoking the fires of anger, or suffering in agony with our stomach twisting into knots, at times we have the quiet suspicion that we may have brought our problems upon ourselves somehow.

What if we hadn't done that one thing? we wonder. What if we had chosen a different behavior instead? We wince internally as we recognize that we may have taken certain actions to hide from potential discomfort, shirk our responsibilities, or avoid confrontation. Perhaps we weren't entirely honest with others or were consciously striving to manipulate the situation to get what we wanted. Beating yourself up for past mistakes can make it difficult to practice self-love and self-care. If you're going to be kind to yourself, you must first forgive yourself for anything that needs forgiving. Forgiving yourself is, in itself, an act of love.

Many people believe that if they forgive another, they're saying what was done to them was okay. They believe if they forgive, they now have to let that person back into their life. This is false. Forgiveness means you decide to let go of the anger and resentments caused by past transgressions. It means you stop living your life based on old hurts and start living from *who you are today* and not what someone did to you last week, last month, or last year. Finally, forgiveness is the secret to *releasing* yourself from the offender, because as long as you remain angry and resentful, you are tied to that person emotionally.

There are so many elements to forgiveness that one could write an entire book about it (and many people have). The following is a simple exercise that will get you started on the path of forgiveness.

A FORGIVENESS EXERCISE: SET THE OTHER PERSON FREE

- Choose one person who you are still angry at and have not forgiven.
- On a piece of paper make a list of the all the things they did that have hurt you. Be specific.
- Bring that person into your mind and acknowledge them as an imperfect person, just like the rest of us.
- For each item on your list, repeat the words "For doing ___ to me, I forgive you. We are all imperfect beings doing our best."
- Try not to judge yourself for how "well" you forgive. If you're unable to forgive at the moment, give yourself compassion and acknowledge yourself for the *intent* to forgive.
- When you've gone through the whole list, get rid of it.
- Repeat as necessary.

JOURNAL QUESTIONS

How do you feel now, compared to how you felt at the beginning of the exercise? What progress did you make? Where do you feel lighter or more open in your body or in your heart?

_____

_____

Did you find that you also need to forgive *yourself* for how this conflict unfolded? If so, repeat the exercise, but this time, using yourself.

_____

_____

We might need to forgive someone over and over again until it really sticks. If you've tried forgiving yourself or others but still feel intense emotion, you might benefit from more information on the subject. Many books offer a step-by-step guide, along with awe-inspiring stories of people reaching out to each other. For a spiritually based approach to forgiveness, check out Colin Tipping's *Radical Forgiveness*.

WORKING ON YOUR BELIEF MACHINE

Everyone has an inner dialogue that runs constantly throughout the day. Unfortunately, most people's dialogue is full of self-criticism stemming from false beliefs about ourselves that were created during childhood, such as:

- I'm not doing it right. I never do anything right.
- I shouldn't eat that. I'm already fat.
- I'll never be able to accomplish that. I'm not smart enough.
- I'll fail like I always do.
- He'll never love me enough. No one will.

It's impossible for you to feel calm and at peace when your inner dialogue is full of blame, shame, and criticism. So first things first, alter that dialogue!

"How?" you ask. Some experts say that 95 percent of our behavior comes from our subconscious patterns and programs, which are formed between infancy and five years of age. During that time, we soak up messages from our environment without a filter, unable to discern whether they are true or false. We're in the theta state of brain activity (one of the most impressionable states) two times a day: upon waking up and right before falling asleep. As mentioned earlier in this book, saying positive affirmations during this time is one of the simplest, easiest ways to begin changing self-defeating beliefs about yourself, other people, and life.

DAILY ROUTINES TO CREATE CONFIDENCE AND POSITIVE MOMENTUM IN YOUR DAY

You know how dieting doesn't really work? Sure, if you want to lose a few pounds of water weight, it does. But if you want to achieve long-term health, you need to change your lifestyle by including exercise and healthier eating habits. Well, it's the same with self-love. You can't just say, *Okay, if I repeat loving thoughts for a few weeks, I'll finally love myself.* We know, life *will* get in the way and you'll just forget about a lot of what you're learning here. We hope you'll allow yourself the opportunity to practice your newfound tools off and on for *years.*

Are you willing to consider a lifestyle change that includes tending to your needs? That may sound intimidating, but it's really as simple as altering your daily routine to include some loving actions. Below are some ways to start implementing this kinder, more nurturing approach.

- Brief meditation, prayer, or expression of gratitude. You can do this before you get out of bed in the morning or in the shower. Think about three things in your life that you're grateful for and voice appreciation for them. (Your health, family, a roof over your head, a secure job, food in the cupboard, close friends, etc.) Name three every morning, no matter how simple. Don't worry about repeating yourself.
- Reading or watching something that will always get a laugh out of you. Laughing releases endorphins that give you a natural high.
- Bed yoga
- Setting a positive intention for the day, using an affirmation, or reading an inspiring quote. You should have no problem finding an inspirational desk calendar to keep by your bedside. Wake up, flip the page and be inspired.
- Right after lunch, take a moment to check in with yourself. Are you feeling tense from the day or are you calm? Take some deep breaths, do some visualization or a short meditation.
- Take a moment before dinner or right after work to again check in

with yourself. Do you need to take a couple of minutes to center yourself? Bathroom breaks are *great* for taking some "me" time!

TAKE IMPERFECT ACTION TOWARD YOUR DREAMS

Another method that might help you build self-esteem is to get out there and accomplish something you've always wanted to do. As we saw above, we hold a variety of beliefs about not being good enough:

> *"I'm not flexible. I could never be a ballerina."*
> *"I'm just not creative or talented enough. I could never be an artist."*
> *"I always wanted to play the drums, but now I'm too old."*

Just the act of taking action and *trying* can have an incredible impact on how we feel about ourselves. You might just find that you don't *have* to have innate talent in order to draw, because with enough practice, anyone can do it! So, what's something you've been wanting to try but have been too afraid or haven't made the time for? Go on. Call up a partner in crime, or if you're too mortified for your buddy to see you in a tutu, go it alone. But go!

CHECK YOUR THINKING

POTENTIAL NEGATIVE BELIEFS

In addition to the limiting beliefs you listed above, here are some more examples of negative beliefs about your self-worth you might not realize you have. Put a checkmark next to any you can relate to.

- Something is deeply wrong with me.
- I'm a loser.
- I can't show anyone my real self.
- I'll never make this family work.
- Everyone leaves me eventually.

- I'm not smart/creative/talented/accomplished/in shape enough.
- I'll never have enough money.
- People can't be trusted.
- People always take advantage of me.
- I'm not worth making an effort for.
- I wish I could be someone else.

What are your thoughts about what you checked off?

_____

_____

_____

INCREASING YOUR POSITIVE BELIEFS

It's possible to dramatically improve the quality of your life by deliberately increasing the number of affirming beliefs "automatically" available to your conscious and unconscious mind. Use the following mantras or affirmations on a daily basis, inputting them into your subconscious twice a day or during a focused meditation. Your choice!

ACCESSING YOUR SUBCONSCIOUS—TWICE A DAY

Contrary to outdated opinion, we actually *can* reshape long-standing, subconscious beliefs. Repeat the affirmations (listed below) to yourself during times of extra stress or, for best results, for a week or two upon rising or falling asleep. During those two times in particular, you are in a theta brain state and your subconscious mind is at its most impressionable.

MEDITATION: FEELING GOOD IN YOUR OWN SKIN

Follow the steps listed for Meditation in Section Two, *Power Tools*, to guide yourself into a nice, relaxed state, then silently repeat any of the following mantras. Take as much time as you need and let any other thoughts that come up for you float by and fade away. If you find yourself drifting off into a state of "argument" with an affirmation, gently refocus your attention, return to the statement and enhance any feelings of softness, warmth and expansion in your heart. Continue until you feel better...

POTENTIAL POSITIVE BELIEFS

Choose two or three that resonate with you and mentally repeat each one, as you breathe slowly and deeply.

- I am brave.
- I am empowered.
- I am deeply loved.
- I am capable.
- I have nothing to prove.
- I know myself.
- It feels good being me.
- I'm grateful for my life, exactly as it is right now.
- I am worthy and enough.
- I'm perfect just as I am.
- My body is beautiful and serves me well.
- I can achieve whatever I put my mind to.
- I'm trustworthy.
- I trust myself.
- I forgive myself for mistakes I've made.
- There are no mistakes, there are only results.
- I'm a work in progress and that's okay.
- I'm lovable and loving.
- I deeply love and accept myself.

CHAPTER 13
BOUNDARIES: MAKING PROGRESS
(overdoing and unprotected vs. clear, consistent boundaries)

WHERE THE WALLS AND WINDOWS SHOULD BE

When we last spoke about boundaries in Chapter Six, we examined some of the ways we might be unknowingly contributing to our own misery through inconsistent limits and overdoing for others. In this chapter, we're going to help you pinpoint the areas in your life where your boundaries are lacking, and walk you through how to create healthy ones. We'll show you how clearly communicated limits and consequences can improve your quality of life and protect you from negative, outside influences.

The list below highlights some common areas where boundaries are usually needed, but are often absent:

- **Privacy:** It can be difficult to have privacy when two households are connected by kids, who easily share the happenings at one house with the other. A lack of privacy could also range from children sneaking into your bedroom and rummaging through your drawers or asking about your income and expenses, to the other woman entering your home when she picks up the kids, even when she's been asked not to.

- **Communication:** We've all experienced being disrespected at one time or another. Most of us are in too much shock at the moment to think of a decent response, but afterwards more than a few choice words come to mind. We can remove ourselves from people who are verbally aggressive with us, but when the aggressor is a member of your dual family, it's not so simple. Or perhaps the opposite is true: you're not faced with directly aggressive behavior, but *passive*-aggressive behavior, such as important information being withheld from you to create an unwanted consequence.

- **Problem-solving:** You're expected to solve problems that aren't your responsibility. Stepmoms are often expected to do a lot of the parenting, even though it's not their job. They are at high risk for developing strong resentments if they think they're being taken advantage of. Similarly, if mom is being told she needs to include stepmom in parenting decisions or that she should communicate with stepmom instead of dad, she's also likely to develop ill will.

- **Possessions:** Your possessions are disrespected. From a stepchild breaking a delicate crystal that's been in your family for decades to someone using your shower towel or make-up. A mother might feel as if she's being disrespected when clothing she's purchased for the kids is not returned back to her house. (Clothing is a big hot-button topic between households.)

- **Authority:** Having input into decisions that affect you. This can range from scheduling to visitation to school issues to medical treatments to practically every issue under the sun! Discipline in particular is a source of conflict in many families. Who decides what the house rules are? Who implements them? What happens when house rules are disrespected? Opportunities for disagreement run rampant because we all want to feel a sense of competence and control as authority figures.

HELPING CHILDREN BECOME SELF-RESPECTING ADULTS

We spoke at length about problems with overdoing for others in Chapter Six and how easy it is for women in particular to slip into this behavior. We can remind ourselves of the opportunities we are *taking away from others* to keep ourselves on track in this area. We can also hold up a positive vision of one of the most important goals we have in our divorced families and stepfamilies: to turn our young, impressionable children into skillful, competent adults who take pride in themselves.

What do we want to model for our children? What kind of adults do we want them to be? If we can help our kids and stepkids internalize the following principles, they'll be way ahead of the game in life:

- **Stop believing in the magic parent fairy:** When you grow up, you will only be judged on *your* performance at work, there will be no one there cleaning up after you. We do our kids a disservice by helping them escape the pressures, failures and learning experiences of responsibility. Even very young children yearn for self-sufficiency.
- **Know how to work hard:** Don't be afraid of using elbow grease. Don't cut corners. If you don't know how to perform a skill, ask. You're not a victim because you have to work hard.
- **Take care of what you have:** Everything starts out brand new and can often be returned back to that state with hard work (see above). Stop coveting *more*. Know the value of what you already own and take good care of it.
- **Know how to make a contribution:** It's not enough to only clean up after yourself. In life, you will have to do for others over and over without it being "fair." Don't keep score and know how to contribute to the common good without expectation of a reward.

If children are consistently allowed to avoid developing a sense of personal responsibility, we will create adults who either feel entitled to not work hard or who feel shame and fear over their lack of knowledge and hide from situations where something difficult might be asked of them. This is a recipe for stunted adulthood, something no parent or stepparent wants for their child.

If we're going to help our children step up, then we must learn how to step back, so they can do more.

FIVE STEPS TO CREATING HEALTHY BOUNDARIES

So how does one do it? How do you communicate your healthy limits to those around you? What if things go wrong? For starters, if you pay attention to how emotions manifest themselves in your body, you'll get a good sense of where you might need to create a new boundary.

Let's walk through the steps required to create healthier limits:

1. Identify the symptoms of your boundaries that are currently being violated or ignored.
2. Identify the irrational thinking and beliefs by which you allow your boundaries to be ignored.
3. Create new beliefs.
4. Create the boundary.
5. Communicate your boundary.

Now it's time to learn more about each of these steps.

1. Identify The Symptoms Of Your Boundaries That Are Currently Being Violated Or Ignored

Remember when you wrote about parts of your life where you had "leaky" boundaries in Chapter Six? Ready to try fixing one of those life areas right now? Flip back through your journal and choose one problem or boundary that you already know isn't working well.

What area would you like to work on? What bothers you about this situation the most? How does this issue feel to you physically?

_____

_____

2. Identify The Irrational Or Unhealthy Thinking And Beliefs By Which You Allow Your Boundaries To Be Ignored Or Violated

Remember the Belief Machine exercise in Chapter Six? Refer back to it for help with this step. Here are some potential reasons for poor boundaries and examples of unhelpful thoughts, based on an article written by Mary T. Kelly, M.A (used with permission).

Ask yourself, *Am I practicing inconsistent boundaries*:

To keep the peace?
> *I need to be the strong one here, since I'm better at the emotional stuff than my husband.*

To avoid the conflict?
> *If I start speaking up about what I need and want, I'm just going to stir the pot and make everything worse.*

To get the ex-wife or stepmom to like you?
> *Maybe if I could just win her over by taking the high road and showing her what a good person I am, a lot of this conflict would go away.*

To look like the good guy?
> *I can't stoop to her level, so I always have to seem like the nice one, the calm and clear-headed one, compared to her.*

To make sure the stepkids love you?
> *I just need to bite my tongue and not ever get mad or lose my temper. The last thing I want is to seem like a hard-ass in front of the kids. And maybe if I'm the "cool" stepmom, they'll accept me and love me.*

To stay on the kids' good side?
> *They've been through a hard enough time with the divorce. I'm just going to love them all the way into good health and healing as their mom, no matter what.*

To be the perfect stepmother and wife?
> *I'll show my husband how different I am from her. I'll show him he made the right choice in marrying me. I'll do such a great job of loving him and meeting his needs that we'll stay together. I'll show her that I'm a better mother, and that I'm more loving, caring, and consistent.*

To be the perfect mom and wife?
> *I'll show her I know what I'm doing and that the kids will always prefer me, no matter how much she tries to be 'the cool stepmom.' I'll do such a great job with my second marriage that she'll regret being stuck with him. I'll show them both what a healthy family unit looks like, something they'll obviously never have.*

To make life easier? To ensure the smooth, yet elusive "blended family"?

If I try hard enough, I can create love, harmony and acceptance between us all.
To avoid rejection?
If I make people mad, they won't like me.

What are some examples of unhelpful thoughts you've had?

_____

_____

3. CREATE NEW BELIEFS

Ask yourself "What is the opposite statement for each unhelpful belief I've listed above?" Throughout this book, we've talked about the power of turning a negative statement around and focusing instead on a positive affirmation. In this step in particular, you give yourself permission to meet your own needs.

Examples of new beliefs (based on the examples above) might be:

"I need to be the strong one here, since I'm better at the emotional stuff than my husband" becomes *"It's okay for me to step back and let others handle their responsibilities, even if they are struggling."*

"If I start speaking up about what I need and want, I'm just going to stir the pot and make everything worse" becomes *"I deserve to have my needs addressed, even if it causes temporary discomfort or upheaval in my family."*

What are some other examples of new affirmations or positive beliefs you *could* have?

_____

_____

4. CREATE THE BOUNDARY

Now let's look back at Step #1 and choose one area where you can see a boundary is needed. *What do you want to have happen instead?* Brainstorm some potential actions you might take in response to a boundary violation. As much as you may not want to communicate with the other person, you must let them know that you do not accept their behavior by making a clear request. This is made up of two parts:

- a direct request
- what you will do if this doesn't happen

Use the following formula to create your boundary:

"I'd like you to (behavior change). If you continue to do (unwanted behavior), I'll do (your consequence)."

For example, a stepdaughter is using her stepmom's make-up without asking. The stepmom says, "Katie, I'd like you to ask me before you use my make-up. If you use it again without asking, I'm going to start locking my bathroom door and you won't be able to borrow it at all."

Here, she has told Katie what behavior she would like changed. Then the stepmom told her what *she* will do if her stepdaughter continues the unwanted behavior.

You do not need to engage in a lengthy conversation with the other person when you communicate your intended consequence. You don't need to get them to accept or approve of the reasons for your request. You can just inform them of your new boundary and go about your day.

> **Brynn (divorced mom/stepmom):** *"I implemented a boundary with my husband's ex when it came to her talking poorly and making jabs about my husband to me. It just made me uncomfortable and I wouldn't 'allow' anyone else to talk about him the way she did. So I put on my big girl pants and told her, 'I know he frustrates you, but I'm just not willing to participate in that kind of banter with you.' She agreed to its inappropriateness and when she tried a couple times after that (I had let her for so long!) I just told her, 'You know I won't go there.' Now she very rarely ever does."*

What positive change are you shooting for? What are some potential consequences you could implement for boundary violations? Which one seems most viable? Choose one.

_____

_____

5. COMMUNICATE YOUR BOUNDARY

People may react to you in one of three ways after you've made a request:

- Option A is that they accept and respect your boundary and don't repeat the same boundary violation.
- Option B is that they appear to accept and respect your boundary, but then attempt to cross the boundary again, hoping they'll get away with it (because you either let it slide or you weren't paying attention).
- Option C is that they directly refuse your request and let you know they have no intention of doing as you've asked.

It's scary to think that standing up for yourself might mean people won't like you or they'll see you as the commonly labeled "evil stepmother" or "crazy ex-wife." But if you want to be successful with boundary setting, it's imperative that you stick to your word, even if your fears about repercussions have you shaking in your boots.

Look back at Step 4 and have some actions ready to implement if the other person decides your boundary doesn't mean squat to them. You can expect some pushback after you've communicated your boundary. After all, no one likes to be told that things are going to be different from now on, so this might be a good time to have a friend on call, in case you need some emotional encouragement.

If boundaries are a new concept to you and the thought of implementing them makes you shudder, then start with a small boundary, one that you feel is easier to implement, where you don't expect as much resistance from the other person. You can also start by creating a boundary with someone you feel safe with. Let them know this is new for you, it's scary, and you'd like their support.

IN THE WORDS OF OUR READERS

Leila (stepmom): *"I implemented a boundary when I asked my husband's ex-wife to please keep all requests between her and my husband. It had gotten to a point where she would Facebook message me about small, trivial things. I feared that if things continued that way, there would be a lot of resentment on my part from being constantly put in the middle. She didn't take it too well at first, but things are much better now. She goes to my husband for everything and the middleman (me) has been eliminated. I'm much happier, not always feeling stressed and anxious waiting for the next shoe to drop. I think she is much happier too, because I think she feels that my husband is doing his 'part' when an issue arises."*

J.B. (divorced mom): *"I had problems with my ex-husband not respecting me or my time. He would call and come by my house all the time. He would leave things on my front porch. I finally let him know that it was not acceptable. I would only answer a call or text or email if it was a direct question or communication regarding school, doctor's appointments or anything of that sort. I would not discuss our marriage or child support (his desire to stop paying somehow entered every conversation) and I stuck to that. If he tried to bring things like that up, I stopped writing back and didn't respond. We switched to school pick-ups and drop-offs because he could not be on time when we met and could not have our kids ready when I picked them up. I'm much happier now (even though I do have to re-establish the boundaries from time to time)."*

N.H. (stepmom): *"There was a situation a few years past where my husband's ex-wife and her husband at the time were taking my stepchildren on a long road trip. My husband and I were out of town and were riding our motorcycle, so we couldn't hear the calls coming from her to ask if they could come and grab the Gameboys for their trip. They decided to stop by our house and* when they realized we weren't home, proceeded to enter the home and send the kids to find the Gameboys to bring along. We didn't find out they had entered our home without permission until the following week. It bothered us that she would just come into our home and tell the kids to take something out without first having our permission. (Unfortunately this wasn't the first time this had happened.) My husband called her right away and let her know that she could only come into our house when invited. She was a little upset and didn't really understand why it was such a big deal. It may not have been if we had had a different/better relationship, but she had been rude and disrespectful to me and of my boundaries in the past. Now she totally understands that she is not allowed in our home without our invitation."

Alissa (divorced mom): *"My ex-husband's girlfriend had caused issues with my daughter's medical treatment, so after many chances, I implemented my boundary that she was not to be involved in any shape or form. I also went to the extreme to get the law and medical staff behind me so I could stop her from even trying to get involved."*

Anonymous (stepmom): *"Whenever I would send out an email to a group of parents for something I would be responsible for organizing, my husband's ex-wife would reply to me only with complaints, criticisms, scolding, etc. So as a boundary I stopped including her by email and when she figured it out, my husband told her she would only be let back onto the list if all her replies were to the entire list. It worked!"*

D.A. (divorced mom/stepmom): *"My ex-husband used to walk right into my house. Even after I moved in with my new fiancé, he continued to do so (at my fiancé's house). I asked several times for him to stop, but he didn't. I ended up locking my doors before he was to arrive. After a few months, he got the hint and doesn't come in before he is invited. Interestingly enough, he stopped calling* *me 7 times in a row when I didn't answer too. Another way I set boundaries was to have exchanges be at the school so we had little contact. I send updates via e-mail to both he and the stepmom so he can't say I didn't tell him something or that he 'forgot'. The conflict has been severely minimized. We have also used the help of a co-parent coach to help him realize that it's not my responsibility to remind him of everything. A good co-parent coach can go a long way. This stuff is a lot of work!"*

Regardless of the boundaries you set with the other party, there will be times when they will just flagrantly do what they want to. When they cross a boundary, you always have the option to either accept or reject their behavior. You can't control them, but you can remove your participation or assistance, as in the example for Step #4.

How can you take care of yourself if you receive a negative response to your boundary? What are some additional actions you can take if someone violates your boundaries?

_____

_____

HOW TO STOP OVERDOING OUT OF "LOVE"

In Gary Chapman's book, *The Five Love Languages*, one of the love languages he describes is "Acts of Service." People who fall under this category feel loved when someone completes a task for them and they tend to show their love for others this way as well. Acts of service are a common love language for men, as they are natural providers and it feels good for them to *do* for their families by making a living, repairing things around the house, fixing a problem, etc.

But for women, they're sometimes *giving* for other reasons, such as the Feminine Martyr Complex we introduced in Section One. Examples of this are stepmoms who often help out their husbands because they have something to prove: that they're a good homemaker and a better wife than the ex. Moms may also have something of their own to prove: that they can do it all themselves or show the stepmom how much better they are at relating to the kids. Neither of these mindsets set you or your family up for your success. You must give away some of the responsibilities you've taken on.

As we mentioned in Chapter Six, so many of these tasks that were originally done from love can easily become expectations on the part of others. Now our contributions go unappreciated and we see others not stepping up like we know they should. So how do we detach with tolerance and compassion while keeping our hearts open?

The answer is to delegate, which is yet another exercise in asking for what you need!

EXERCISE—HOW TO DELEGATE TASKS

1. Think about your daily routine, from the time you wake up to the time you go to sleep. Make a list of each action. A small sample might include:
   * waking up the kids
   * making breakfast
   * taking out the trash
   * grocery shopping
   * cooking dinner
   * doing the dishes
   * taking the dog for a walk
   * putting away clean laundry
   * giving the little ones a bath
   * reading bedtime stories

2. Next to each action, write down who normally completes that task.
3. Now go through the list again and look at which tasks have your name next to them. Assign each task a score, 1 for tasks in which it is absolutely necessary for you to be the one completing it, and 10 for the tasks that could easily be given away to someone else in the family, especially if it falls under "Great Life Skill to Have."
4. Beginning with the 10s, start assigning them to different family members.

5. Continue delegating your tasks until you get to a place where you're comfortable and don't feel so overwhelmed with the amount of responsibility on your plate. Experiment!

There's no need to rush this exercise. If you can delegate just one task initially, that's a great start. Baby steps are okay here. The more you share the load, the more comfortable you'll get. As your stress level decreases, your entire family will benefit.

Feeling stuck? Not sure what or how to delegate to others? Try these questions:

JOURNAL QUESTIONS:
BRAINSTORMING OVERDOING AND DELEGATION

What are you doing for others that they could be doing for themselves?

_____

_____

Where are you struggling with responsibilities that are genuinely yours? What tasks do you absolutely detest doing? Are you willing to "trade" tasks? Is someone else in the family *better* at certain tasks than others?

_____

_____

What do you want and need to let your partner, the other parent, the stepkids, or your children begin doing? Where are their areas for growth and increased responsibility? Where are you *taking away* from them by *doing for* them?

_____

_____

What does it mean to you if you stop overdoing? What about pushback and negative reactions or the potential discomfort of upsetting people? What's your fear here?

_____

_____

HOW TO ASK LOVED ONES FOR SUPPORT

For those of you who aren't very confident in your communication skills, we offer some sample language for requesting changes and delegating. It can be hard to ask for what you need. Sometimes seeing an example helps you envision what it might look like or sound like for you to do it. Here are some ideas:

> "Honey, I know we've all been really stressed lately. Can we sit down and talk about how possibly rearranging some of our responsibilities might help with that?"

> "Honey, I'm feeling really overwhelmed right now. I'd like to look at some alternatives to me picking up the kids from school one or two days a week. Freeing up that time for me would really decrease my stress level and would provide me with the ability to better support you and the rest of the family."

> "Kids, since you're getting older, it's time for you to start taking on more responsibility. Here is a list of things that keep our household running smoothly. Can each of you to choose one that you want to be responsible for?" (You can add more later.)

Now it's time to take a closer look at the thoughts churning around in your head.

CHECK YOUR THINKING

POTENTIAL NEGATIVE BELIEFS

Here are some examples of negative beliefs you might not realize you have. Put a checkmark next to any you can relate to:

- If I say "no" to anything, I'll look like a jerk.
- If I ask for more help, others will reject me.
- I can't voice my needs when my partner is already so overwhelmed.

- I'm selfish if I put my needs ahead of my family's.
- I have to be the family maid or no one else will do it.
- No one cares about what I need.
- I signed up for this, so I have no right to complain.
- It's my fault that I can't figure this out in a way that makes everyone happy.
- If I get pushback, I'm doing it wrong.
- I have to do what everyone wants me to do.
- My family will fall apart if I stop doing everything.
- I will be stuck living in a pigsty if I step back.
- I have to be needed to be loved.
- I don't deserve to want more than I have.
- These people are hopeless!

What are your thoughts about what you checked off?

_____

_____

_____

INCREASING YOUR POSITIVE BELIEFS

It's possible to dramatically improve the quality of your life by deliberately increasing the number of affirming beliefs "automatically" available to your conscious and unconscious mind. Use the following mantras or affirmations on a daily basis, inputting them into your subconscious twice a day or during a focused meditation. Your choice!

ACCESSING YOUR SUBCONSCIOUS—TWICE A DAY

Contrary to outdated opinion, we actually *can* reshape long-standing, subconscious beliefs. Repeat the affirmations (listed below) to yourself during times of extra stress or, for best results, for a week or two upon rising or falling asleep. During those two times in particular, you are in a theta brain state and your subconscious mind is at its most impressionable.

MEDITATION: FEELING GOOD IN YOUR OWN SKIN

Follow the steps listed for Meditation in Section Two, Power Tools, to guide yourself into a nice, relaxed state, then silently repeat any of the following mantras. Take as much time as you need and let any other thoughts float by and fade away. If you find yourself drifting off into a state of "argument" with an affirmation, gently refocus your attention, return to the statement and enhance any feelings of softness, warmth and expansion in your heart. Continue until you feel better…

POTENTIAL POSITIVE BELIEFS

Choose two or three that resonate with you and mentally repeat each one, as you breathe slowly and deeply.

- I establish healthy limits for myself and my family.
- By taking better care of myself, everyone benefits.
- I model great self-care for the kids.
- I'm allowed to say "no" to others.
- It's okay if not everyone likes me.
- Every grumpy mood will pass.
- Friends and family support my self-care.
- Giving the kids responsibilities yields other gifts for the future.
- I deserve to ask for what I need.
- I have the power to improve things I don't like.
- I am strong enough to withstand rejection.
- I can release control.
- I create my own personal validation.
- It feels great to love myself.
- I thrive on managing my time and resources.
- I'm comfortable delegating life's tasks.
- My place in my family is secure.
- We all pitch in together in our little family community.

- I am deeply worthy.
- I feel safe asking for what I need.
- I allow others to learn and grow.

CHAPTER 14

CONCLUSION

If you've made it through to the end of the book without skipping chapters, we want to congratulate you. Looking at yourself with a magnifying glass is never easy, but we're hoping you've already started reaping some of the benefits. Our wish is that you've created a permanent, positive shift within yourself by working through the tools and exercises here.

Perhaps you've come to realize that all is not as it appeared and that you have more power to generate personal peace than you once thought. Maybe you discovered that you've been holding on to some resentments and judgments that can now be released. If nothing else, we hope you see that you are not alone and have many other fellow travelers with you on this journey.

We'd like to leave you with a few words from our readers, since they're the ones living these issues. We've learned the most from them and hope their words will inspire you to shoot for the best in yourself, even though it might be hard at times.

> **Katie**: *"I just wanted to say thank you for the last few years. You definitely turned my high-conflict situation into a success story. Three years ago, I never would've dreamed that the mom would become a regular babysitter for my children, that we would sit with each other at ball games, or that she and my husband would be able to get through a* major *custody schedule change without lawyers, mediation and court rooms!"*

> **Aimee:** *"Thank you for changing my view on everything, especially my counterpart. Thank you for making our abnormal family and*

circumstances feel normal. Thank you for helping me grow, learn, and strive to be a better addition to our family."

Kelly K.: *"Thank you for teaching me that just because it's the norm to hate your counterpart, it doesn't have to be that way. I spent a lovely day at the ball diamond with the mom, my future husband, my stepson, stepdaughter, my parents and my sister, and everyone got along. For the first time in five years, the mom wished him a Happy Father's Day."*

Amber: *"I don't have a friendship with either of the moms in my life and feel comfortable with that. I know I haven't done anything wrong and we all have our own journey. I get along with one and have learned how to distance myself from the high-conflict one. It is good."*

Jeri M.: *"I don't have the words to express what I have learned. Unreasonable hate removed from my heart. Knowing my feelings are okay. Peace in my home and peace in all my tumultuous relationships."*

Lauren T.: *"I've gained friends. I've gained perspectives I truly wouldn't get anywhere else. I've gained compassion. I've gained the ability to know it's okay to take care of me. I've gained more than I think I'm even aware of. It infiltrates into much more than just things regarding the mom, my stepson and my future husband. It's applicable to all aspects of my life and for that, I will forever be grateful."*

Whether it's learning how to treat yourself more lovingly, how to not let that immediate fight-or-flight response determine your actions, or spending some time strengthening your boundaries, our aim has been to introduce you to some life-changing concepts that you will make your own. Whatever it is that you'd like to improve upon, make sure to also cut yourself some slack, because personal growth is a marathon without a finish line. If all goes well, we'll live to be little old ladies who are still refining our abilities to live happier, more loving lives right up to the very end!

If you haven't made as much progress as you'd like, take solace in the fact that you're on your way. Even the smallest change in your mindset that results in you being less stressed, anxious or angry will have a domino effect on everyone else in your life. Your children and stepchildren's lives will be the better for it. Your partnership will benefit. You really *are* changing your family's future by modeling personal responsibility, forgiveness, kindness, love and grace.

We wish all of you the very best and we hope you'll stay in touch!

OTHER RESOURCES

For more hands-on support, please join us online at SkirtsAtWar.com and NoOnesTheBitch.com. We'd love to have you join our Facebook pages, workshops and private forum. Jenna Korf is available for private coaching at StepmomHelp. com or JennaKorf.com. You can keep up with Jennifer Newcomb Marine's latest projects at JenniferNewcombMarine.com.

THANK YOU

Thank you for buying and reading *Skirts at War: Beyond Divorced Mom/Stepmom Conflict.* We hope that you found the book helpful and relevant to the issues you are working on! If you have a success story you'd like to share with us as you experiment with the strategies in this book (or spot an error), we'd love to hear about it. Please write to us at JenandJenna@noonesthebitch.com.

As independent authors, we don't have a marketing department or massive distribution in bookstores. If you enjoyed this book, please help us spread the word and tell a friend, share via social networks, blogs or post a review on Amazon or Goodreads.

Sign up for our mailing list at SkirtsAtWar.com and NoOnesTheBitch.com if you'd like more tips on creating happy and healthy dual-family relationships.

Thanks and much love,
Jennifer Newcomb Marine and Jenna Korf

ACKNOWLEDGEMENTS

This book is the result of two years of stops and starts. It's not easy to write a book with another person, especially when our two personal journeys have been so different. Luckily, we found that we work exceptionally well together, brainstorming, and filling in the gaps for each other's ideas. Plus, not many people can launch right into an old-lady sheep's voice at the drop of a hat on the phone. We make each other laugh so hard it's a little scary.

First and foremost, we'd like to thank the members of our NOTB community. So many of you shared your hearts and souls with us. Your stories helped us bring this material to life in a way we never could have done without you. We know your words will serve as a comfort to many new readers who are discovering these challenges for the first time. Many of you graciously gave us your permission to use your full name, but in the interests of protecting you from any future, unforeseen circumstances, we decided to only use initials for last names or eliminate them altogether. We hope you understand.

Several of our community members also served as early first readers. You worked with us on some crazily tight deadlines and your feedback and suggestions for improvement were invaluable. We owe a huge debt of gratitude to: Laura Bonura, Jessie Marie Castonguay, Heather Coleman Voss, Beth Daniels Olkowski, Gail DeVore, Mollie Ellis, Anita Inglis, Angi Kolthoff, Dina McCausley, Kathy Patrick Seligman, and Katie Price.

Jennifer would like to thank family and friends for their love, support and encouragement, especially my daughters, Madeleine and Sophie; my parents, Roger and Sylvia; and my brothers, Brad and Ross. Warm thanks to Rebecca Lincoln, Pippa Gaubert, Penny Van Horn, Crista Beck, Jennifer Ferland, Liz Alexander, Kai Woodfin, Karen Owens and Nathan Havlick. All my dear friends in my long-time writers group, the Austin Writergrrls. Special warm and affectionate thanks to Kaili, Liza and Zane. And to the man who changed my life, Rhett, honey, a million hugs and kisses. You have my heart.

Jenna would like to thank: My friends for being there every step of the way. My stepsons, Zak and Mason, for putting up with me as I tried to figure this whole stepmom thing out. My husband, Mario Korf, whom without (for obvious reasons) this book never would have been written. But also for being my biggest supporter and best friend and for surprising me on a daily basis with your willingness and ability to grow as a person, father, and husband. There's no one I'd rather take this journey with. And most importantly, my mom and stepdad, Caren and Bud Berman, and my dad and stepmom, Richard and Lori Rothstein, for raising me in a happy, healthy, conflict-free stepfamily. I'm forever grateful for that gift.

A shout out to sci-fi writer William Hertling for his helpful book, *Indie and Small Press Book Marketing* and to Joel Friedlander of TheBookDesigner.com for demystifying the process of self-publishing.

And last, but certainly not least, grateful thanks to our bang-up self-publishing team: Damon Za and Benjamin Carrancho for a book cover that gave us chills the first time we saw it and beautifully formatting the book (contact them at www.damonza.com) and to Amy Eye and Jeanne Goshe for proofreading and editing, respectively. You saved us (and any errors that remain are our own)!

ABOUT THE AUTHORS

Jennifer Newcomb Marine is the co-author of *No One's the Bitch: A Ten-Step Plan for Mothers and Stepmothers* (GPP Life, 2009), which was co-written with artist Carol Marine, stepmom to her children. She writes for the NOTB blog, *The Huffington Post* and is also a public speaker. She's the mother of two daughters, an honorary aunt to her children's stepbrother, and lives in Western Oregon with her partner, four teenagers and three dogs.

Jennifer's been featured on *The Dr. Phil Show*, *The Washington Post*, Canada's *Globe and Mail*, *Publisher's Weekly*, *Library Journal*, *Psychology Today* and numerous radio shows and interviews. For her latest projects, visit JenniferNewcombMarine. com.

Jenna Korf is a certified Stepfamily Foundation coach and works with stepmoms and couples to help them overcome their stepfamily challenges. She's a regular contributor to *StepMom Magazine*, blogs for *The Huffington Post* and NOTB and has been featured on CNN.com.

Jenna lives in upstate New York with her husband, two teenage stepsons and an adorable pup named Astro. For more information on working with Jenna, visit her at StepmomHelp.com or JennaKorf.com.

Mario Korf is a technical writer for Salesforce.com and has published articles on motorcycling, spearfishing and topics in between. His hobbies cannot easily be counted.

Made in the USA
Lexington, KY
10 June 2014